Roni's Story:
A Daughter of Africa

Roni's Story:
A Daughter of Africa

VERONICA WALKER

Paperback: 978-1-63767-046-0
eBook: 978-1-63767-045-3
Library of Congress Control Number: 2021900136

Ordering Information:

BookTrail Agency
8838 Sleepy Hollow Rd.
Kansas City, MO 64114

Printed in the United States of America

CHAPTER 1

The car groaned up the last of the hills and as we rounded the corner, the Zambezi valley lay spread out before me at my feet. I had come to the edge of the escarpment and below the land stretched out flat, away into the distance where the heat haze obscured the horizon. The browns, reds, and blues of Africa changing and intermingling as the clouds drifted across the sky throwing their shadows down onto the parched earth.

The end of the dry season was slowly drawing to a close but before the rains came the land would endure the build up of the heat. The long golden grasses at the side of the road shed their seeds like a shower of silver drops as the car created a stir in the air. The dust seemed to linger long after I had passed. As I sank down to the valley floor the heat enfolded me like a blanket. The breeze that came through the open window of the car was hot but did nothing to dry the sheen of sweat on my bare arms. The scent of the dust laden bush was strong and heady.

Moira whimpered as she sweated in her pram at the back of car. I prayed that she would stay asleep until we came to the customs post and then passed over the silver bridge across the Zambezi river into Rhodesia.

At long last, I was coming home to stay. My mind roamed back over the years trying desperately to find a reason for our failure. We now had no money or prospects and my marriage lay in tatters. So many years ago I had crossed this valley on my way north, young, enthusiastic and ready for adventure. I had followed blindly where fate, in the shape of my husband seemed to be leading. Family background that shaped and influenced me and made me what I am must have lent a hand to that same fate.

Perhaps it went further back to the time when both my parents came to this vast land, met and then decided to spend the rest of their lives together.

They had met in a very small Portuguese village across the border from the new colony of Rhodesia. Dad had been sent by his bank in Pretoria to open a branch there and Mum, after having nursed in the Great War in East Africa, had taken a post in Umtali. She was sent across the border to help with an epidemic that was devastating with the population. What my father's attraction was I don't know. Mum must have met many men during her active service, who might have made ideal husbands but she fell in love with Dad and married him in Pretoria where he had been recalled as Bank Manager.

Here Mum practiced her social graces with tea and dinner parties for the Bank's customers and in every way became an ideal Bank Manager's wife. Their first daughter, Ann was born in 1924 and the family looked set to lead a comfortable and sedate life.

But the call of the bush was too much for Dad. Who wanted a wear a collar and tie every day when a whole continent of freedom waited for those who were brave enough to take the chances it offered?

Without consulting Mum, he invested all his savings in a cotton farm in Mozambique. Taking his wife and baby daughter into the wilds of Africa the family started to cotton farm. Apart from the fact that in all probability he knew nothing about farming the first rainy season washed his first crop and and all his capital down the river.

The family walked off their farm with what they could salvage and retired to Rhodesia to lick their wounds.

There is, in the family's archive of memories, a photograph, taken several years before I was born, that seems to typify this period in the history of my family. The photo is of a motor car being pulled along a dusty road, by a span of oxen. The year is approximately 1928. Resplendent in the driver's seat is my father, a pith helmet on his head, and a big grin on his face as if he realized the sense of the ridiculous in the situation. Beside him sits my mother, her face hidden by a large parasol, may be not quite so amused. In the back seat, in solitary splendor is my sister Ann. But perhaps the most startling thing about the picture is that the oxen are being led by an African. So much for motor power!

This picture seems to me to tell a story not at first apparent from the faded images it displays. The car must at one time have been new and shiny. It was now rusty and mud laden, and of course at one time it must have traveled bravely over the rough roads under its' own power full of confidence. There had been no need for the span of oxen then. How sad that, like the car, my parent's dreams had turned to dust.

In Rhodesia conditions were not easy. The colony was very young and jobs were more or less non existent but Dad fell in love with the country and, as so many did, succumbed to the dreaded "Gold Bug". This is a disease where the chance of 'striking it rich' from the discovery of a bonanza of gold has ensnared many a stronger soul than him. He was never to recover from it, and although he did at times work on farms or as an accountant, the old pick and pan were never very far away. He was always prospecting, looking for the elusive rainbow. But perhaps, besides the gold, there was also the lure of the bush, its' solitude, perfume, and beauty an enslaving mistress.

Dad was farming outside Rusape when their second daughter Mary was born in the little country hospital there. But presumably this farming venture failed as I was born in Umtali three and a half years later. Apparently, the family had been on another farm and had to vacate it with all their goods and belongings. Dad parked Mum with two children and another ready to make her entry into the world, on friends. How humiliating it must have been for them but it says much for the people of the colony who were always ready to help each other in times of need.

After my arrival Mum did not recover as expected not really surprising after all the worry, and the hard life. With the help of Dad's family we were all packed off to South Africa where we lived with Dad's sister in Cape Town. Dad remained in Rhodesia but it was a year or more before finances had improved enough for the family to be reunited. Then it seems that he once again went mining

On one occasion Dad was in partnership with an Afrikaner on a mine called The Poor Man's Luck. Mum was living in Umtali at that time, with the children, and sewing bunting flags for a living. These flags were used to decorate the small town when the Prince of Wales later to become Edward VIII visited the new colony.

The shaft on the Poor Man's Luck had been newly blasted and when the dust had settled the chief African miner was lowered down in a bucket by a rope. After a considerable delay Dad shouted down.

"What's the matter? I suppose that we have found gold" "Yes" came the reply, "Manningi mari" (Lots of money).

When Dad had been lowered into the mine he could not believe his eyes. The wall of rock facing him glittered in the light from his lamp. He shut his eyes, counted to ten and then opened his eyes again. Yes, there was definitely gold shining and winking at him from the rocks.

Samples of 'gold' were hurriedly collected and loaded into his battered half ton truck and the two partners rushed into Umtali to the Assayers office. Grins splitting their browned faces and dressed in their muddy work clothes, they rode down Main Street. News of their great strike spread like wildfire. The Mayor congratulated them and everyone not least Mum started to celebrate. However the balloon was soon burst when the report from the Assayer's office proclaimed that the samples were a good example of pyrites or fool's gold and of little monetary value. Once again the family was out of funds.

The family dutifully followed Dad around from various farms and mines. Looking back I often wonder how my Mother managed to put up with the grass huts and shacks that she turned into homes for us. A typical homestead in those days, for us, was two or three separate huts made of tree trunks with thatch roofs, not always waterproof. The walls would in time be covered with mud and a floor was constructed of cow dung mixed with water and clay. This when dried gave a firm highly polished covering which could be patterned if one so desired. On several occasions sheets had to be hung above the beds to prevent the borer dust from falling on us while we were sleeping. The borers were small hard backed insects that ate the grass on the roof and produced a fine dust that filtered down covering all underneath in a red film. The legs of all the furniture stood in small tins that were filled with paraffin to prevent the white ants or other creepy crawlies from climbing up.

However there was no method to prevent spiders, lizards, snakes and such like from wandering in at will.

Outside the huts, the ants made their mud passageways up the sides of the walls and as children it was our job to continually knock these down with a stick. We would watch the pale, albino insects scurry down the holes in the earth from which they came, only to emerge the next morning to restart their tortuous way up the wall again.

All water to be used for washing or drinking had to be boiled in case of bilharzias as it came from the nearby river. The kitchen was always separate from the living rooms in case of fires. If we stayed long enough, two huts would be joined in the middle making a passable sitting room.

Mum always kept chickens and made a garden. She sold what we did not consume ourselves and hoarded the proceeds of the sales. Dad of course treated her ventures into the 'money markets' with a slightly amused male contempt but on various occasions I heard him ask,

"Any chance of a few bob for petrol?"

When conditions became too bad or money ran out Mum returned to her nursing and supported the family.

Amongst my earliest memories is that of a rather large gold mine, called The Reliance, of which my father was the manager. Mother ran a boarding house for the single miners employed there. During this time on the Reliance mine we three girls although relatively young got up to all kinds of mischief. Ann was a weekly border at the convent in Umtali and Mum taught Mary, at home, but we had all weekends and school holidays together.

Mary's school desk was on the veranda, outside the dining room where the miners came for their meals. At lunch time she would sit at her desk watching through the window and mimicking one miner in particular who sat just inside the room.

To our young minds he was an old man. His name was Mr. Jorgeston and he sported a very bushy discolored moustache that covered his top lip with hairs. He appeared to have some difficulty in getting his soup spoon to his mouth as the spoon would be raised and lowered several times before the soup was finally strained through the hairs and deposited in his mouth. Then, with great delicacy, he would remove the remaining vegetables from his moustache with his forefinger and pop them onto his tongue. It became a favorite pastime for us to repeat this action and it never failed to send us into fits of laughter.

The Reliance Mine mine was situated on the main road from Umtali to Salisbury but traffic in early '30 was very light and certainly the cars that existed did not travel at a very great speed. Not far from the entrance to the mine the road took a deep dip. Having secured a large, very dead snake we tied a piece of string to the head, laid out the snake at the side of the road and taking the end of the string we hid in the tall grass on the opposite side of the road. At the approach of a car coming down the dip Ann would slowly pull the snake across the road. The car invariably stopped, the driver alighted and began to 'kill' the snake. Ann would then stand up.

"What are you doing to my pet snake?" she would ask.

The driver would splutter apologies and we found the situation hilarious

The snake would have had to be very dead before we had touched it as none of us would have dreamed of knowingly going into the vicinity of a live one. Fear of these reptiles was instilled into us at an early age.

For a while life seemed secure but the cattle belonging to the farmer on whose farm the mine was situated, started to die mysteriously. It was discovered that the huge chimney from the mine smelter was spewing out cyanide with the smoke and this settled on the grazing. The mine was closed within 24 hours throwing both black and white workers out of work.

Whenever the family traveled it was always by half ton truck. Our parents sat in the front and we three girls alone in the back would dangle our feet over the tail board. If we passed through a drift or small river we would all stretch out to see who could touch the water with her bare toes (we rarely bothered to wear shoes) until on one occasion Mary outdid herself and slipped off the truck. Much banging and shouting drew Dad's attention and Mary was rescued from the muddy water none the worse for her ordeal. But sadly our parents now alerted to our games forbade the lowering of the tail board of the truck on future rides.

On the closure of the Reliance Mine Mum became the matron of a children's convalescent home up in the Vumba mountains of the Eastern District. Dad was also employed there in looking after the rather extensive acreage surrounding the property. The home catered for youngsters from poor families who had been ill and required extra care. The Vumba mountains were considered very beneficial as the air on the mountains was clear and cool. The hillsides were covered with lush forests, under which grew swathes of green fern. The grass on the mountains between the forests was short and thick and the whole area became famous for its dairy products and fruit.

Plantations of wattle trees were planted. Their bark was used in the tanning of leather and in the spring, when the yellow furry blossoms were thick on the branches their perfume wafted over the mountains and a yellow haze seemed to surround the trees.

Mum had a magnificent flower garden and was quite renowned for her watsonias, a flower somewhat like the gladiola but with longer spikes of bloom. These flowers grew in the front of the house to an average of five feet and bent their long spears of purple bloom as the wind played through them rippling their blossoms like waves in a sea of color. The scent of freesia can take me back to the damp forests even to this day, as they grew here in profusion but they were not indigenous having originally been imported from the Cape by some flower lover in years past. They had flourished and multiplied and now propagated themselves over the mountains. Protease flourished wild around the side of the mountain where they enjoyed the cold winds that blew there. At this early age the love of flowers and gardening was instilled in me.

The forests of course are the result of the heavy rainfall in the area. As the clouds swept in from the sea to the east they deposited their moisture on these mountains, which are the edge of the escarpment and there were days when the soft damp mist covered the land. It swirled around the trees and all shadows became enlarged, ghostly, and very frightening to me as a little girl. We called this mist 'guti' and it could continue for weeks on end. At these times we were not allowed to stray from the house as it was so easy to get lost. But when the sun did appear the countryside sparkled and the air was pure and fresh and scented with the perfume of numerous wild flowers, foremost amongst which was the small yellow curry flower.

Strangely the inmates of the home, for the most part, consisted of boys and from all accounts I led the gang and handed out discipline to any boy who did not conform. Mum recounted how on one occasion while I was dealing out punishment with my fists to some unfortunate boy another youngster queried

"Do you need any help Roni"

"No" I replied "I can manage him myself"

What a dreadful child I must have been – a fact that my fair curls belied! It could be that this was evidence of the stiff necked pride I had inherited but to be kinder to that little girl of so long ago, I would rather call it self reliance.

Because the road up to the mountains was so very precipitous and was really no better than a dirt track we received very few visitors. Therefore the monthly visit of the European Police Inspector and the African Constable was a great occasion. They arrived on horseback and usually stayed the night. Their horses would be rested and both men would luxuriate in a hot bath, eat home cooked meals and sleep in a soft bed after having being on patrol in the bush for up to three weeks. The Inspector would be accommodated in our house and the Constable disappeared into the huts of the African compound, a place of intrigue for us youngsters but which was strictly out of bounds.

Before leaving they gave rides on their horses to all the children accompanied by calls of

"Me next" or

"Please just one more turn around the house"

When they finally rode away in their starched and shiny khaki uniforms amidst much waving and cheering, we felt a little isolated and lonely.

Another regular visitor was Father Seed the Catholic Parish Priest from Umtali. He made the journey once a month. He was a small very nervous man and the trip up the mountains must have been a real trial to him. He said Mass in our home for the few Catholics in the district, then after having a meal he would wend his slow way back to Umtali. I'm sure that he heaved a heavy sigh of relief once he was safely down the mountains.

Our house was situated below a hill called Castle Beacon which rose up into the sky on massive granite rocks. In places some of these rocks had tumbled down and formed gigantic buttresses. The rocks themselves, some as big as a house were of a blue grey color and were covered with orange and white lichens and mosses.

From the top of Castle Beacon the view stretched away to infinity. The purple ridges of the far away Chimanimani mountains lay to the south and in the East the Mozambique planes were encircled by the foothills of the plateau. Standing out of the blue haze one mountain closely resembled the head of a mermaid lying in the water, her profile turned towards us and the ends of her hair floating in the blue mists.

Nearer but while still facing to the East was a mountain with its end sheared off; the remaining cliff face a vertical drop of several hundred feet. According to African folklore the mountain had fallen because the tribe that lived at its' base had refused food to a wondering witch and had chased her away. The witch had cursed them and caused the mountain to topple and smother the whole village.

Later the local tribe made a practice of throwing their prisoners as sacrifices to their Gods, from the mountain top onto the sharp rocks below. It was reputed that on some still nights, when the mists lay thick over the forests the cries and moans of the dying could still be heard. No wonder the area was considered haunted by the local Africans!

The mountains stretched away to the north right up the side of Africa, but nearer to home was Inyanga, too far away for us to see but another lush farming area. Below us to the West and hidden from our view by the hills the little town of Umtali nestled in the valley.

Around the side of Castle Beacon and a few miles distant from our home, was the house of a very old couple called Myberg. Mr. Myberg now well on in years was very deaf but had been quite famous as a spy for the British in the Bore War. How he managed to drive his car remains a mystery as he could not hear the engine and frequently forgot to change gears.

Their house was built of stone with a very low roof much like the Scottish crofters' houses. The walls inside were blackened by smoke from the fire that was kept continually lit as both the old people were crippled with rheumatism. I remember the sound of the rats scurrying above the ceiling that neither of the couple could hear. They were looked after by their African cook, Adam, who was almost as old as they were.

Mr. Myberg grew fruit on his property amongst which were plums which to me seemed to be the size of a small orange. The skin and flesh of these plums was so dark red, as to be almost black and when you sank your teeth into the sweet flesh the juice ran freely down your chin soaking the front of your dress. We children were always turned loose in the orchard when we went to visit.

Mr. Myberg was known to have spells of 'Mental imbalance'

"Quite bats!" Dad would say

When Mr. Myberg had to go into Umtali on business or to get supplies, accompanied by the ever faithful Adam, Mrs. Myberg would stay with us. She was a big woman with an ample bosom and dressed in flowing long white gowns. On one occasion she appeared with a kitchen towel wrapped like a turban around her head with a beer bottle top stuck in the front of it to resemble a jewel. She strode up and down the dining room reciting Shakespeare.

"To be or not to be." Her deep voice thundered through the room.

We children sat around, our mouths hanging open in awe.

Radios were very few and far between and it goes without saying that delivered newspapers were non existent. The nearest post office was in Umtali 25 miles down the mountains. However we did have the telephone, when the storms had not destroyed the telephone lines. The line was a party one and operated on a system of different rings, and anyone could listen into the conversations. At about 6.30 every evening a farmer some miles away and who was in proud possession of a wireless, as the radio was known then, would give a special ring on the phone and would relate the day's news as cleaned from the broadcast, always beginning with the words

"Here is the news as far as I can make out between the atmospherics".

The damp, cold air affected Dad and he became ill with rheumatism. He must have suffered a great deal of pain and was eventually sent down to Hot Springs in the low veld. Here warm sulphur springs gushed from the earth and an enterprising couple had opened a guest house. The waters had been dammed to make a swimming pool, and although the accommodation was in grass huts the steamy sulphur heat was very soothing and beneficial. Unfortunately Dad would never be able to live on the Vumba again and when he had recovered from his illness, he became the manager of a Dairy farm outside Beira in Mozambique, for a short period while the owner was ill.

Mum remained on the vumba with us children and Dad's place was taken by young man whom Mum mothered.

Although isolated as we were Mary and I contracted Scarlet Fever. I was obviously the more robust child and recovered with no ill effects. Not so Mary. The disease left her with a heart condition and she became desperately ill. It was imperative that she be looked after in a hospital. Luckily the convalescent home was empty at the time and Mum nursed Mary in the Umtali hospital. The Doctors stated that the altitude was too high for her and that she should be removed to sea level. She could be accommodated in a special children's hospital in Capetown.

Our family had no money for expenses like this and the Rhodesian State Lottery, which had been running for several years by then, came to our aid and paid all her expenses even to the trip by boat from Beire to Capetown. It was considered that she was too weak to undertake the train journey. She was to remain in Capetown for the next two years.

While Mum was nursing Mary in Umtali, Ann and I spent a few weeks with Dad in Mozambique. The farm must have been right on the coast as I well remember swimming in the warm sea. We spent the day near an old wreck of a boat that had run aground and the goats grazing nearby ate my jersey.

Apart from this the only thing that I can remember of the holiday was the chicken that, every day was served up stewed and stringy by Dad's cook. How I longed not only for Mum but also for her cooking.

Because of Mary's long illness Mum had had to resign from the convalescent home and Dad in the meantime took out license and started a small gold mine which he called "The Ann Claims". This mine had a one stamp mill, for crushing the ore that was extracted from the banks of the Odzi river. The mine was actually situated on the farm belonging to the Deal family and in the years to come, in Salisbury, our two families would remain friends

Once more we lived in grass huts. It was here that I learnt to pan for gold from the mud of the river. The excitement that I felt when, having whittled the mud down from a full pan to a few grains at the bottom of it, I first saw the bright shiny flecks of gold winking up at me was tremendous. I carried those grains around in a small bottle of water for days until they were replaced by a small nugget that wonders of wonders, I found amongst the rocks. That there was alluvial gold in the river there was no doubt but there just was not enough to mine.

The life was very hard on my Mother as we were very isolated and the Africans in that area were very primitive. Any old clothes that we could no longer use were given to the workers on the mine who sold them on to the local population. Mum always wore a boned corset, a habit left over from her strict Victorian upbringing. On one occasion, having thrown out an old one we were very amused to find an African boy, herding some goats, decked out in Mother's old corset. On the ends of the suspenders he had attached clothes pegs which he had painted in a bright red and on these he carried his flute and other objects that he might have need of during the day.

In one instance, at the age of 7, Mum took me into Umtali to the dentist a distance of some forty miles. I cannot recall how we got there but on our return we were dropped at the side of the main road and had to walk a considerable way through the bush to the river across from which the mine was situated. There was no road in and obviously the family did not possess any transport at that time.

When we reached the river it was only to discover that it was in flood and was impassable. Cupping our hands and shouting across the roaring of the water eventually brought Dad to within hailing distance.

The conversation went something like this.

"Hullo Dear. Did you have a good trip?" called Dad.

"Yes. Roni has had two teeth extracted, but we can't get across.", Shouted Mum in return.

"Well you'll have to wait for the water to drop." was the unhelpful reply.

"But it is getting so late. The sun will be down soon". Mum complained.

"Try and make it to the drift at the Deal's farm and I'll meet you there" was his advice.

So Mum with my hand held firmly in hers, turned away and we walked another couple of miles to the Deal's farm in the growing dark. She must have been frightened and worried for the safety of both of us. I often wonder how she put up with this kind of treatment. I never heard a cross word pass between my parents.

Eventually Dad lost the gold reef on the "Ann Claims" and the family was once again out of funds. I secretly think that by now Mum had had enough. Taking me, she begged a lift to Salisbury in the front of a transport lorry belonging to A.B. Roberts, an American. Mum had looked after his son in the convalescent home some time previously and Bobby his wife was a frequent visitor to the home. In years to come I was to meet up with the family again when they were farming in Karoi, and Fred, my future brother–in–law was employed by them at one time. It seemed that ours' was a very small world.

CHAPTER 2

In Salisbury, Mum borrowed some money, rented a large house on Jameson Avenue, and with typical resilience started a boarding–house which she called "Villa Anthony" in honor of St. Anthony. This she ran for the next twenty years and the family became static for a change. Once established, Ann came up from Umtali and Mum brought Mary back from CapeTown. Dad joined us and began work as an accountant, a position that Mum probably organized. I began proper school then at the age of eight, Mum having taught me intermittently for a year.

Once more at home, Mary continued to improve in health but we were told that she had to be looked after. She was not allowed to do any sport and in order to get enough rest she had to go to bed early every night. As we all shared the same room Ann and I had also to retire early. We would spend the hour or so before going to sleep singing. I often wondered how the diners appreciated our young voices raised in song, often out of tune.

Mary made the most of her illness often making me carry her books home for her unless there was some boy that she could persuade to do it for her. In that case she would dismiss me with a flick of her hand.

"I don't need you Roni" she would say.

She then proceeded to look wan and wistful so that the poor youngster would feel obliged to offer his help. There were no flies on Mary.

We had been in Salisbury for only eighteen months when war broke out. On that fateful Sunday morning the whole family and many of the borders crowded around the ancient wireless and listened to the British Prime

Minister inform us that war had been declared. Mum cried and Dad, possibly in order to hide his feelings gave his usual grunt and went to tinker with his car. I couldn't understand what all the fuss was about. England seemed very far away to me.

Rhodesia was among the first colonies to follow England's lead and declare war on Germany. There was a rush of young men, both black and white, to enlist, train and in time leave for the front, many never to return. When the first troop train left Salisbury station the whole town turned out to see them off. The Police band played marching tunes and everyone except the mothers, wives and girl friends cheered. The men were all excited to be going on an adventure for, as was believed, a few months. The train whistle blew a shrill blast, steam hissed onto the platform and the train slowly drew away. Hands that had been firmly grasped through the windows drew apart. The cheering reached a crescendo. The smiling faces on the train became indistinct and faded. As the tail lights of the last carriage disappeared from view down the track it left an almost intangible emptiness behind it. The cheering and the band came to an abrupt halt and only muffled sobs disturbed the silence that fell over the station. The crowd now in sober and somber mood drifted slowly away.

The country girded itself to withstand invasion.

Rhodesia was and always had been staunchly British. We had at times been accused of being more British than the British. We were immensely proud of our heritage and although we, as a people, no longer called the United Kingdom 'Home' we carried on the traditions of the British Empire. The Union Jack flew from all over Government buildings and 'God Save the King' was played or sung at the beginning of any public event, while everyone stood to attention. Any youngster fiddling during the Anthem was severely reprimanded. We were taught to hold principals, play by the rules, to stand upright, and fight for what was right.

Mum joined the Red Cross and organized First Aid posts. Dad was in the Civil Defense and a fire watcher. Endless meetings were held as a result of which sirens were erected on the church steeples most being the tallest buildings and gradually rusted away. Trenches were dug in any place of spare ground to save us from the bombs, but as they soon became awash in the rain, Salisbury suffered an epidemic of malaria. So they were filled in again the sirens being rusted. Even blackouts were tried. There was talk of gas masks being issued. Why everyone thought that Germany would be interested in invading Rhodesia is now hard to imagine but such was the hysteria at that time. Eventually life returned to its usual slow pace.

And then the "Blue Plague" hit us. England sent out recruits to be trained as air crews and pilots for the Royal Air force. At first they were welcomed with open arms and were taken into our homes in the usual hospitable manner of the community.

Unfortunately after several unfortunate incidents of assault and rape, hospitality was not so quite forthcoming. Rhodesian troops had to be confined to barracks at one time in order to keep them away from the 'Poms' whom they threatened to beat up, and young women were advised not to venture out alone. Eventually things settled down and many of the R.A.F. married Rhodesian girls, Ann being one of these war brides. Far too many of these boys in blue remained in Rhodesia in graves after having killed themselves during training.

"The Ville" being situated within easy distance of the Air Force Headquarters, six of the newly arrived "Poms" were billeted with us, and Mum proceeded to mother them all. She sent parcels of oil, tea and sugar to their families every month and kept up a correspondence with their mothers where possible. They all became members of our family and when Dad died they carried his coffin at his burial. John who was to become Ann's husband was one of these original six men. The others kept in touch for many years after the war was over.

Rhodesia also became a center for Italian Prisoners of War taken in the North African Campaign. Several heavily guarded camps were set up in relatively isolated areas. In time many of the prisoners were released into the care of local farmers on parole. Several proved to be expert builders and craftsmen and there were many examples of their expertise to be found from reservoirs to small highly decorated chapels dotted around the country. Many outlying communities owed their very well engineered and constructed roads to the Italians. Many stayed in the country after the war and their families came out to join them.

We also became hosts to Polish Refugees, the vast majority of whom were women. These unfortunate people had been taken prisoner by the Russians. In return for the promise from the men to form an army, to fight for the Allies, the women had been sent overland through Russia, India and Africa, eventually arriving in Rhodesia travel weary and without any news of their menfolk. The inevitable committees were formed, by local population, clothes collected and the refugees settled into brick built camps around the country. Employment was found for them wherever possible. We had three young women billeted with us and Mum employed one, Maria, to help in the boarding house. Maria was an expert dressmaker and a very hard worker. I well remember some of the dresses that she made for me and she also gave me lessons in sewing. It was many months before these people received any news of their men. Eventually information did trickle through that their army had been engaged in the battle for Monte Cassino in Italy and had suffered many casualties. At the end of the war the Poles were given the choice of returning to Poland or remaining in Rhodesia, and I believe that the majority voted to return to their homeland. One wonders how they fared in the turmoil that ensued in that country.

My father was a very large man over six feet in height and with a sizeable paunch. His head, except for a narrow band of white hair under the dome, was bald. We called his head a fly's skating rink, although we had never seen a skating rink except in books. Because of his baldness he always wore a nightcap in bed much to the amusement of us children. He had had his teeth removed many years before but had never been able to afford to replace them. However he could eat anything from apples to biltong, a dried meat. I cannot remember my father with his teeth as we entered our teens. Perhaps because of this he always carried a pen knife in his pocket in order to pare a snake. This knife was used for all manner of things, from trimming his nails to scratching rocks in his continual search for gold. I doubt very much that it was ever washed.

Dad purchased a very second hand Chrysler car, already of vintage years. This car boasted a canvas hood, Perspex windows that had to be buttoned on, four doors and a long seat at the rear. The top of the backrest of the front seat was usually occupied by various family pets amongst which, at one time was a muscovy duck, called, of course, Donald. Unfortunately the engine of the Chrysler had a peculiar device. This was a small tap on the carburetor that had to be turned on so that the petrol could get through. Of course this should have been done before setting out but Dad made a habit of neglecting to do this and we would be half a mile down the road when the engine would cough and die.

"Turn on the petrol" Dad would call.

As young girls we were never allowed to fraternize with the African staff and we were never taught any African Language which I recognize now as a great mistake. The African, considered to be inferior in intelligence had to learn English! Boys had a much freer life style. We girls were never allowed out by ourselves after dark. In fact it was a very male dominated life with few openings of employment for women.

But we did have our bicycles and in groups, we youngsters boys and girls, would cycle miles on picnics during the school holidays. As we grew older a lorry was occasionally hired and we could then venture further. Mermaids Pool about 30 miles from Salisbury was a favorite haunt. Here a river split out over a very large rock forming a large pool below. We would slide down the rock on old inner tubes from car tires and spend all day basking in the hot sun and swimming. We all swam like fishes. As the water had come over the rock it was considered to be Bilharzia free.

During the holidays we usually had a party on the veranda of 'The Ville'. The red cement floor would be polished to a bright shine, the half walls surrounding it covered with cushions and the old gramophone wound up, ready to play the 78 records. Mary was usually the one who got things moving and organized these parties. We all dressed up on these occasions, the girls in long dresses and the boys in their school uniforms or smart sport coats. There was always a smattering of uniforms as the boys we knew grew up, left school and joined the armed forces. We also had friends amongst the Air Force. We danced to the popular tunes of the day having to run over to the gramophone and rewind it whenever it slowed.

However our life was not all play and every evening one of us girls was expected to serve out the cold meats and sweets as they were ordered by 'The Boarders'. Laundry had to be counted out and in and we sometimes found ourselves cycling down to the market which was on the other side of town, to purchase the week's supply of fruit and vegetables. Mum usually did this chore but we did help during the holidays. The old Chrysler had been sold on Dad's death and our only mode of transport was by bicycle. In order to transport the provisions home one of the African servants would follow with a wheelbarrow and when it was full he returned home with it.

To raise money for "Our brave allies The Russians", once a year, during the war, a great fete was held in the center of the city. The whole of one of the longest streets was turned into a fair with stalls and there was dancing in the street. The merriment lasted all night but sadly my curfew was 10:30 p.m.

Balls and dances were also held to raise funds for the Red Cross or other worthy causes and Mary and I with other young girls were often called upon to sell balloons or cigarettes at these functions. We were dressed up in saucy costumes with short skirts and frilly blouses but sadly being under age we were not allowed to take part in the dancing no matter how many times we were asked. The temptation to disobey was very strong as we thought that we were really the belles of the ball.

My best friend, at that time, was a girl called Jean Gilchrist. Her family farmed just outside Salisbury and her father ran a business in the town. Jean and her sister came home with me from school every day for lunch and were collected by their father at the close of business at the end of the day.

Mary and I sometimes spent the odd weekend on their farm. At that time they owned a couple of horses and occasionally I was allowed to ride them under supervision.

On one occasion Mary had gone to the farm without me and had asked if she could ride. For some reason she was mounted onto a very nervous horse which reared. The girth broke and Mary tumbled to the ground. She was unconscious and was taken into casualty by ambulance. After x–rays a fracture was discovered in her lumber spine.

Mary spent several weeks in hospital and when she came out she was in a plaster cast from her armpits to her hips. This stayed on for a further six months and once again she qualified as an invalid! But Mary had a lot of initiative and on an old treadle sewing machine she would sit for hours on the veranda and make handbags. These she would sell and by the time she was allowed back to school had made herself a good deal of pocket money. From here she progressed to an excellent dressmaker.

Besides the Air Force Headquarters, a very large flying school was built at Cranborne in Salisbury. Hundreds of young English men were trained here before being sent back overseas as pilots and navigators etc. The accident rate was very high and in order to relieve the pressure on the overcrowded hospital wards, the Red Cross opened a convalescent home to accommodate these men until they were able to resume normal duties. Experienced staff was very difficult to find and Mum became the Matron of this home. How she managed to combine both the boarding house and the convalescent home is difficult to imagine but she did for a year or two.

Being very staunch Catholics we three girls were educated at the Convent school. This school was run by the Dominican who carried on the traditions of those first sisters who came up to Rhodesia by ox wagon at the beginning of the century under Mother Patrick. The majority of the nuns were of German nationality. The war years must have been extremely hard for them. They were cut off from their families for the whole period and there was no communication with them. They could hardly turn a deaf ear to all the anti German propaganda that was in all the newspapers and on the wireless. At one time rumors were rife that the good sisters would be interned in the camps that were erected for members of hostile nationalities. Common sense did however prevail and the nuns were left in peace. Besides the schools that they ran in all the main centers of the country, they also staffed many mission stations, without their services education and health would have been dealt a hard blow.

The standard of education at the convent was second to none, possibly because the Nuns would not allow anyone to sit for the exams unless they were confident that the pupil would pass.

Sport however was frowned upon, although it had to be taught. The good sisters were not in favor of seeing young ladies displaying their legs on the hockey fields or indeed their bodies scantily clothed at the swimming pool. This to me was a pity as I was rather good at both sports but the Convent always came bottom of the league in any competition.

The Catholic religion was instilled into us. We had instruction daily from catechism to latin hymns, adultery or anything slightly pertaining to sex omitted. Even the Old Testament was not considered suitable reading material. Once a year there was a dance with our brother school St. Georges College. I think this was to teach us some social graces. Everyone was expected to attend once they had reached the senior years. The hall was decorated with bunting and Nuns stood guard at all the doors and patrolled the grounds incase some erring couple should disappear into the dark. To me these occasions were real purgatory. I knew very few of the boys and being tall for my age could usually look over the head of all of them.

For most of the long evening I would grace the wall endeavoring to look quite uninterested in the proceedings. If I was honored by being asked to dance it was a quick dash up the hall a turn and a dash back all the while my arm being pumped up and down, not even in time to the music, and the boy's other sweaty hand clamped firmly on my back leaving a dark damp damp stain on my dress.

It was decided by the Nuns, that I would never make academic material and that my only hope would be to get married and have children. On one occasion a very frustrated nun, having failed to install the rudiments of algebra into me shouted

"You have no brains Veronica, only common sense".

However, more due to the persistence of the Nuns than any ability on my part, I did sit and achieved very good passes in the Senior Cambridge school examinations. I have also held some very good jobs during my life!

Ann had left school before Dad died and after a short spell as a clerk in the Air Force she became a student nurse. Mary (three years younger than Ann) left school three years later and joined the Police Force. While still at school, and under pressure from Mum, I enrolled as a student V.A.D. in the Red Cross. There for a period all four of us were in uniform, even if mine was only a twice a week effort.

The end of the war finally came and life changed once again.

The Rhodesian forces slowly trickled back and the men were once again available to take over the jobs that the women had been doing. As Mary's employment was considered to be a male occupation she was then out of a job and she became a student Radiographer. The English Air Force started to leave to return to England.

In order to secure a passage on a boat Ann received special permission to get married to her John before she had completed her nursing training. And so with Mary and I as bridesmaids she and John exchanged their vows in the Cathedral in Salisbury. John left for England almost at once and Ann was to wait another year before she was able to join him as a war bride. Ann's leaving nearly broke Mum's heart although she tried not to let us see or hear her distress.

Before I left school Mum managed to purchase a second hand Ford Anglia and after a couple of attempts passed her driving test. We all learnt to drive in this car, me being the last.

On the morning of my momentous test the car was parked across the road from the police station beside an opening for a gate. A few yards up the street was another opening. I was seventeen at the time, rather immature and shy. The tests, in those days, were conducted by the police and I drew a very large redhead policeman who caused my young heart to flutter and this increased my nervousness. He took me through the oral test inside the station. We then went across the road to Mum's car. I found that I was unable to open the door with the key and the policeman obligingly forced the lock. We settled in and as I pulled the starter button it came out of the dashboard in my hand. Now, in the past there had been no difficulty in starting the car.

Nervously, I looked around at the back seat and found several articles that were not there previously.

"I'm mm afraid that we are in the wrong car I sputtered in horror. "Mine is parked beside that opening up there."

The Policeman put back his head and roared with laughter and I shrank further into the driving seat. As we were getting out of this car the irate owner appeared and we gave him a very hasty explanation as to why we were in his car. The Policeman had forced the door key anyway, and I felt that he had to take some of the responsibility for the fiasco! Once settled into the right car we both saw the funny side and we went laughing down the road. At the end of an hours test I had my precious license in my hand but no date with the policeman!

With the return of the Rhodesian Forces the tempo of life in Salisbury stepped up again and there was many a party to welcome the men back home. Wally was amongst these returning men. He and Mary fell in love and became engaged. Mum was against the match and tried to persuade Mary not to marry him. Mary however was adamant and planned her wedding to take place two days after her 21st birthday. Mum bowed to the inevitable and almost broke the bank to give Mary the best wedding that she could afford. They were married by Nuptial Mass in the Cathedral. The reception was held at the town's best hotel Meikles. Mary's best friend and I were bridesmaids.

In no time Mary was pregnant and Barry was born. Within 18 months Marrianne, a daughter, had arrived. But in spite of the ideal family the marriage broke down.

At the age of seventeen my one ambition was to go to a nightclub. Although there was no formal 'Coming out' my family thought that a girl should wait until she was eighteen before wearing makeup or going to public dances. I pestered Mum until she finally gave in. but I was not allowed to go with any of my friends. She chose my partner, who had just returned from the war and was an old family friend. She was sure that I would be safe with him. Well on the way home I had my first experience of fighting to protect my virtue and my partner had a sizeable red mark on his cheek before he left.

The next day when I told Mary what had happened she said

"So he tried it on with you too. He doesn't know when to stop. He also tried to seduce Ann".

This was the ultimate insult. It was like wearing handed down clothes. However, although I refused any further invitations from this man I never told Mum. She might not have agreed to any more dances with partners of my choice.

CHAPTER 3

The next step was to find a career for myself. I had no idea what I wanted to do with my life. To be honest there was not much choice for a young girl.

"I want to do something different" was my constant cry when I was asked what I intended to do with my life.

But what? There just wasn't anything different unless I went to university and that was out of the question as the family finances could not stretch to the expenses entailed. There was no university in Salisbury at that time and let's face it I was certainly never going to shake the world with my academic achievements.

The day after I left school, at the breakfast table, Mum announced

"I've made an appointment for you with the Matron of the hospital" she said, "For tomorrow morning."

Before I knew where I was, I was entered into the School of Nursing in Salisbury, where Ann had trained. Thus did my Mother achieve her ambition that her three daughters would all have a profession and able to support themselves through life.

I entered the Nurses Home with my suitcases and my stomach in a whirl. I had never really been away from home before except for short stays with friends and I was not sure that I wanted to do this thing. The Home Sister, after carefully checking my name against her register, led me up to a room in which were three beds, and rather dull furnishings. The curtains looked as if they had been hung there since the home was built. Until I was more senior I would share with two other girls. The sister closed the door and left me to unpack. All I wanted to do was make my escape back down those dingy stairs and out the front door. I was too shy to enter the dining room and went to bed that night hungry.

The nurse's home was actually very pleasant, surrounded by large trees and lawns. There were two tennis courts and a large swimming pool for use by the staff. There was also a very comfortable sitting room that once a year was turned into a dance hall for the annual ball. No boy friends were allowed beyond the sitting room.

When we went on night duty we changed rooms to a corridor specifically reserved for night duty staff in order that there was peace and quite during the day.

The same system was employed for the theatre staff as they had to be woken at 4.30 in the morning or sometimes even earlier. The junior on the private ward would bring over coffee for these nurses and she also had the key to let in those on late passes. It was a good idea to become friendly with her as she could sometimes bend the signing in times.

However on my first morning, I was not aware of all this and in my new, starched, white, uniform I went straight on to the ward. There was no initial lecture or settling in period and I stood around like a spare part until one of the nurses put a duster into my hand and said

"Start dusting at the bottom of the ward and work your way up. When you have finished there is a pile of bloody linen in the back to be sluiced through before it is sent to the laundry."

I was to spend most of my first three months bending over that sluice basin and my hands, unused to this kind of work, became red and chapped.

When I went off duty I crawled into my bed too tired to think of food. I wondered what had hit me. I had never before had to work like this. It was only the thought of having to tell Mum that I couldn't take the work, that stopped me from packing my bags and leaving the hospital. But gradually my body became used to the regime and as I became more senior and took on different tasks life started to become more interesting. Then my horizon was no longer bounded by the edges of the sluice basin.

I met up with Judy. We had been at school together but as she had been a boarder and I was a day scholar we were not really great friends. It was lovely to find someone that I knew. Judy was feeling the same as I was and we both faced the next day with the same apprehension. In the weeks and months to come we were to provide a shoulder to cry or laugh on for each other.

Judy came from a fairly well off farming family but she was an orphan. Her mother had died when she was still a little girl and her father died just before she started nursing. Judy was now a wealthy girl but her finances were controlled by her older brother. However, he would dole out cash to Judy whenever she came with a hard up story. There were times when I was jealous of Judy who didn't have to budget her meager salary as I did and I'd cast a greenish eye on her wardrobe or the car that she eventually bought while I sewed all my dresses and rode a bicycle. But she was very generous and great fun to be with. We shared many an escapade.

I thoroughly enjoyed my four years training although I constantly moaned and threatened to leave. During our training we worked for a period of three months on a ward but sometimes longer. The hours were from 7.30 in the morning till 8p.m. with four hours off during the day. We had one day off a week and a half day each second Sunday. Night duty was a twelve hour stint when we worked ten nights with three off for three months. All lectures were in our off duty time. There was no initiation period for new nurses. We went straight onto the wards.

As a very new probationer on the Men's Medical ward I found the patients very helpful and sympathetic. After having been given a very quick explanation of how to carry out the procedure I was sent to give a man an enema. Hiding my nervousness, as I thought, I put the screens around his bed, ordered him to turn over and was ready to insert the catheter, when his muffled voice told me

"Right Nurse" he said "When I start chewing, You stop pushing."

His humor put me at my ease and we giggled and laughed as I carried out the procedure to a successful conclusion.

Perhaps the hardest thing to cope with as a new nurse was death. When one has nursed a patient for sometime it is natural that some kind of bonding takes place and we were advised and lectured on how not to get too emotionally involved with a patient. In theory that sounds all very well but one had to grow a very hard skin not to feel any emotion at all. Could I have done something more? I'm afraid I never managed to come away from a death bed without a twist at my heart strings. Worst was definitely the children's ward.

I remember a little girl of two years who died of cancer. She had been abandoned by her family who could not face the thought of her death. We used to carry her around with us whenever we could spare the time and spoil her terribly. At her death the whole ward staff was in tears.

We used to refer to being on duty when someone dies as 'catching' the death and usually tried our hardest to avoid it if all possible. In those days we laid out the patient after washing the body. All orifices were plugged, the corpse clothed in a clean white shroud, hair brushed, false teeth inserted if possible, chin strapped up, and eyes closed. Then we accompanied the porter who pushed the trolley to the mortuary. As most patients seemed to die at night this was not a very pleasant duty as the mortuary was separate from the main building and hidden behind a screen of creaking gum trees.

One of the first deaths that I 'caught' was an old man who died of a cancer in his ear that eventually went to his brain. In his last days his bed was in the side ward of the Men's surgical. This ward had a door to the main passage of the hospital and he used to get out of bed and sprint down this passage towards the entrance, his white split back shirt flipping around his thin body as he ran along. People entering the hospital would stand back in awe and gape. He was surprisingly strong and it took two nurses at least to bring him back up the green tiled passage to his ward. He was past reasoning with and did not understand what we were doing. The stench of the cancer growing out of his ear seemed to waft around him and got right inside my nose. It would linger long after we had secured him in his bed, he had been sedated, and we had moved on to other tasks.

The sense of smell has always been a very strong in me and it was this sense that was my undoing at the post–mortem that we were obliged to attend in our first year. It was not the sight of the body but the stench that arose from it when the pathologist entered the body cavity that caused me to faint for the first time in my life. I will never forget it.

We sat two big exams during our training. The first one was called the Preliminary (Prelim for short) and consisted of anatomy and physiology mainly. We had to know all the bones of the body and name their various bumps and nodules. Also included was the brain and the nervous system. The names of the various parts of the brain would just not sink into my head and I went into the oral with my knees shaking, sure that I would fail. But I wasn't asked one question on it.

The final exams were taken six months before we finished our contract and consisted of written and oral examinations. The examiners were the leading Surgeon and Medical Director plus the Sister Tutor from the General Hospital in Bulawayo. It was a harrowing experience.

Discipline was very strict. No one was ever called by their christian names and woe betides any junior who walked through a door in front of a nurse two weeks senior to her. We were not allowed to be friends with any nurse who was more than three months senior to us. This rule was blatantly disregarded by Judy and me as we became friendly with Trudy, some six months senior to us, from Kenya and a couple of the other girls. I think that the thrill of finding ways around what we regarded as silly rules added to the spice of the friendship.

The doors of the nurses home were locked every night at 10

p.m. but we were allowed a late pass twice a month until 1a.m. Of course as we became used to the system we learned many a trick to get inside the home if we were late.

It seemed to me that I was always up before the Matron, Miss Mulligan, and I could honestly draw the pattern of the carpet in front of her desk from memory. The majority of my misdemeanors were very minor. The wheels of the beds were not straight enough to please the sister in charge or the corners of the sheets were not properly tucked in for inspection. I wondered how the matron of this busy hospital managed to find the time to deal with these petty offences. Obviously there were personality clashes and some trainees came in for more disciplinary attention than others. I was very stubborn and at that time very anti 'the Poms' and I suppose that this showed in my attitude towards the trained staff.

As a junior one was treated as a disagreeable necessity. Most of the trained staff at the hospital were recruited from England and many had served in the war. We called them War Surplus but they were more commonly known as 'Sunshine Girls.' Many had come to Rhodesia to find husbands and thought themselves superior to 'these colonials'. Although they were supposed to be training us they repeatedly stressed how glad they were that they had trained in England and looked down on the Rhodesian training.

Judy and I were both tall girls and were continually being mistaken for each other. Many a time I got into trouble for her misdemeanors and she for mine. We didn't take our reprimands very seriously and would laugh and joke about them.

I found theatre the hardest part of my training. We were on our feet for up to fourteen hours. The day started at

4.30 a.m. when we were required to set up the theatres and sterilize the instruments that would be required for that day. If you were on call you could be up for most of the night and still be expected to be on duty at the regular hour in the morning.

All theatre nurses lived down a separate corridor and all gave off a distinctive odor of ether when they passed you. Because they worked such long hours there was no social life for a theatre nurse. They just sank into bed when they were off duty. The corridor where they had their rooms was aptly named "Virgins Alley".

The atmosphere in the theatres during the operations was intimidating to say the least. While the trained staff and the surgeons would laugh and tell jokes, the 'dirty nurse' (because she was the only one non sterile, in a medical sense) was never spoken to and relied on a series of hand signals from the sister in charge by which she conveyed her wishes.

On one occasion while working as the dirty nurse during a Caesarean section operation, the assisting sister motioned to me that she required a further bundle of swabs. These swabs were squares of absorbent material and were made up in bundles of eight. They were used to mop up the blood and keep the organs within the body cavity moist. After the nurse removed the swabs from the sterile bin with large forceps and deposited them in the bowl of boiling water within reach of the sister she would then write the number on a black board. The number would then be checked at the end of the operation to ensure that none were left in the body cavity.

I had given the sister the swabs and turned around to write the number on the board. Instead of calling to me that she required a second bundle, the sister picked up her bowl of near boiling, bloody water and threw it at me.

I was astounded. My mouth fell open and my eyes nearly popped out of my head. I looked down at my theatre gown, soaked with the bloody water, and the blood clots and globules of fat that now adhered to it. It must be said in my favor that I stayed for the completion of the operation, having the patient's welfare at heart before running from the room in tears. I refused to mop up the water and as a further protest at such treatment, I would not change my gown all that day and finished the shift in the blood stained one, by which time the material had stuck to my skin and had to be soaked off.

The next day I once again found myself studying Matron's carpet for insubordination as I had worn a dirty gown! Although I protested at the treatment I had received, the only reaction I got from Matron was a raising of her eyebrows. I never received nor expected any apology.

We enjoyed Native hospital. This was a collection of wards reserved for the Africans and was grossly overcrowded due in some part to the fact that if a child came into hospital the mother and often the siblings stayed as well. We received a great deal of our experience here although we were only allowed to nurse in the woman's and children's wards. There was only one nurse on each ward and we were forced to make decisions and to deal with emergencies by ourselves. This taught us confidence and self reliance. The actual nursing was dealt with by African ward maids many of them very capable women.

On night duty, in African Hospital, we often made friends with the night duty police and the patrol car would stop and the occupants came in for a cup of tea during their shift.

On one occasion a land rover pulled up at the casualty door and the young policeman ran up to me,

"I've got a casualty in the truck, and I need you to help me get her out" he hurriedly explained.

I dropped what I was doing and joined him at the back of the vehicle

"If you would just take her arm and help her out" he said.

I removed the blanket but as it was dark I could not see into the truck. The smell however, hit me in the face. I held my breath as I took hold of the woman's arm and gently pulled. Her skin came away in my hand and with a scream I jumped back only to find that the young policeman was in fits of laughter.

"She has been dead for about a week" He said. "We pulled her out of the river tonight"

I looked at him in horror and then with my clean hand clamped firmly over my mouth I ran to the toilet where I retched my heart out.

African orderlies worked in the men's wards. These Africans did a three year course and were then sent out to run clinics in the bush. They were for the most part extremely competent, but because their English was not of a terribly high standard their reports were often a source of much delight and amusement to us. One report read,

"Bed 6. Much better night. Had a little jelly and vomited a trifle."

Another classic was

"Bed 12 Medicine given at 6 p. m., and when the train to Umtali all left, and when the train from Bulaweyo arrived. P.S. the clock stopped at 6 p.m."

It must be said the the train whistles from the station could be easily heard at night. Hopefully the trains were on time that night.

There were many strange and unique cases in African Hospital, from huge goiters to malformed bones and we were encouraged to observe these patients. Indeed there were doctors from all over the world who came to update their experience.

We were fortunate to have Dr. Gelfand on our staff who recorded many of the strange cases. He was often to be seen with his camera roaming around the wards.

The Africans who came in from the rural areas had usually already been to the local witch doctor and the staff was hard pressed to undo the harm these ngangas had caused, but all the same many of the African medicines have been proved to be beneficial now.

One such case was an elderly man who had a cancer in the bones of his leg. It was decided by the Surgeons to amputate the limb. However he refused the operation and left to consult a witchdoctor in the low veld. He appeared a year later and proudly displayed his leg, that although scarred, now had no traces of the cancer.

On one occasion an old man was admitted with gangrene in one of his big toes. As it was spreading very rapidly up his foot it was decided that the only cure was to have his foot amputated. It took a great deal of persuasion to get him to consent to the operation and time was running out when he at last agreed.

The theatre was set up for the emergency operation and the patient anaesthetized. Unfortunately at this stage his heart arrested and the Surgeon had to open his chest and do a heart massage. As soon as his heart was once again steady, his chest cavity was closed and the patient returned to his bed. When he woke up he had a large cut on his chest and his toe was still on his foot. Unable to understand what had happened he took the first opportunity to escape from the hospital and return to the bush.

Towards the end of my training a huge hospital reserved specifically for Africans was built in the African township of Harare and at that time was one of the most up to date hospitals in Africa.

We worked extremely hard and played just as hard. Boy friends were plentiful. By the time I completed my training I had become engaged twice and broken it off both times. Mum despaired! Both my sisters had married young and here I was at the age of twenty three and not a husband in sight! She obviously thought that I needed a stabilizing influence in my life.

My first boyfriend had been Chummy. We met when we were both still at school and progressed to engagement when I started nursing. I suppose that as we grew up we changed in our outlook on life and I eventually found him very dull in comparison to the other men that I met during the course of my training. But he was a very good man and stayed a good friend to Mum after I had left Salisbury. His father had started and run the first plant nursery in Salisbury and was responsible for importing the many varied colored bougainvillea that surrounded the town.

Chummy owned a triumph motor bike and I learnt to drive it unbeknown to Mum. I loved the sensation of freedom that it gave me and the feel of the wind through my hair when I rode it. Chummy sold his bike to buy me an engagement ring and I understood how much he had given up when I finally gave the ring back to him.

After a year of playing the field I fell in love with Mac, or thought I did. We courted and went out for about eighteen months. When Mac asked me to marry him I was thrilled but as the weeks went by and he postponed taking me to meet his mother I began to doubt his sincerity and broke it off. It obviously did not break his heart as he was married before four months had passed. I was a little deflated that he had recovered so quickly!

And then along came John! Born and reared in Scotland he had served an apprenticeship as a butcher when he left school and had later become a policeman. This was a reserved occupation and at the outbreak of war he was not allowed to enlist. After two years he was finally accepted into the R.A.F. He trained as a pilot and was then sent out to South Africa with the "Blue Plague" on Training Command for the R.A.F. as a flying instructor. He had had a very comfortable war, never having fired a shot in anger. Back in Scotland at the end of the war he was demobbed and then he returned to South Africa on a tramp steamer.

But with all the returning South African forces, work was difficult to find and so he came to Rhodesia where he once more became a butcher and took a room at "Villa Anthony". He later became a student farmer and progressed to manager of a tobacco farm in Karoi, an area north of Salisbury.

When John came to live at the "Villa" I was still in school gym dresses and the family lost touch with him once he went farming.

One evening after returning from a dance with a group of friends we stopped at Miekles Hotel, as usual, for a last cup of coffee and I met him again. As was natural at that time I invited him home for a meal the next day. John literally swept me off my feet and I thought that I was in love for the first time. I walked around with my head in the clouds and could not see the ground beneath my feet. But John did not reveal his feelings for a few months during which time I spent several weekends at Karoi, always with either a member of my family or Judy. It was just not done that a young girl spend a weekend alone with a man on a lonely farm.

On one occasion John and I cycled to a neighboring farm and borrowed a couple of horses. Although I was not a competent rider I had been on a horse several times but John insisted that we keep the pace to a mere walk. On the return journey I grew impatient and kicked my horse into a gallop. Well I didn't actually want a gallop but more of a trot.

However it only took a couple of minutes for me to realize that I could not control this horse who smelt home and decided that that was where he was going as fast as he could. John followed me shouting to me to pull up. But I couldn't. The beast just would not respond to any amount of sawing on the reigns. Eventually I lost a stirrup and tumbled off. I must have knocked myself out for a few minutes and I came around to the sound of John's voice saying

"What am I going to tell your mother?"

Not very flattering considering the way my head was thumping. Having watched in horror as I had slowly left the horse's back John had jumped off his horse without restraining it and both horses made a bee line for the stables leaving us with a two mile walk home.

As we approached the homestead we saw horses being led around by the stable boy.

"We must get on John" I said "or I may never ride again".

John's horse was the nearest and he took the reigns and started to mount the beast. But the horse had had enough and before John had settled into the saddle it took off. I watched John's bottom waving from side to side as he and the horse topped a small rise and disappeared over the other side. I started to run up the incline sure that I would find John mortally wounded on the other side. The sight of his bottom waving from side to side across the horse's rump was one of the funniest things I had seen for a long time and as I ran I laughed and laughed at the same time frightened of how I would possibly find him. But although he had taken a tumble he was unhurt except for a dent in his pride.

Perhaps I was flattered by the attentions of an older man as he was 13 years my senior and perhaps I was looking for a father figure rather than a husband. He read prodigiously, anything that he could get his hands on, but for preference novels etc. His bookshelves were full of tomes on philosophy and other subjects well above my head. I thought that he must be a very deep thinker. The fact that these books were never opened I missed altogether and I never saw him read them.

John on the other hand was possibly attracted to my youth and sense of fun and adventure. I think that he was also essentially a lonely man at that time. He was very romantic and proposed by letter. Whatever the reason the die was cast.

It was just after this proposal that I once again spent a weekend in Karoi. As I could not find a chaperon to come with me John booked a room for me in the local hotel. On the Saturday night we had dinner with friends of John who ran the local Farmer's Co. Op. and we were rather late getting back to the hotel. It possibly took us too long to walk the few hundred yards from the house to the hotel! When we got there all the doors were locked and I couldn't get in. We walked around the side of the building and found my window but the sill was about six feet above the ground. The window was open and so I climbed on John's shoulders and went into the room head first. It was while my legs were dangling at a very unbecoming attitude out of the window that our giggles and whispers must have awoken the next room occupant who thrust his head through his window and thinking that John was making an exit instead of me forcing a hasty entrance exploded with one word

"Disgusting".

Rather then meet the man next morning at the breakfast table I went without breakfast.

After a somewhat hasty romance conducted for the most part by telephone, as John was farming about 120 miles from Salisbury, he formerly requested my hand in marriage from Mum. I thought this was a huge joke but was not amused when they both persuaded me that a year's separation in England at the end of my training would be beneficial. As I would have to finance the trip myself I was not all that pleased.

The prime mover in this suggestion must have been Mum as I don't think that she was all that thrilled by our unofficial engagement.

CHAPTER 4

Judy didn't need much persuasion to come with me and together we booked our passages on the Stirling Castle sailing from Cape Town to Southampton. The cruise would take 2 weeks. Air travel, at that time was rare and very expensive.

We stood on the platform of Salisbury railway station on a warm evening in March 1953 with our families and respective 'boy friends' around us waiting for the train guard to blow his whistle and cut short the prolonged farewells. Mum had tears in her eyes and I must admit to having mixed feelings about that trip. John, with a confidence that I did not feel, was sure that I would return ready for marriage. Although excited, I felt that if he really loved me he would not be so happy to see me go.

Amid fond farewells and promises to be faithful we boarded the train for the three day trip to Cape town on the very tip of Africa.

On reaching Kimberly, which was a day and a half journey, we were getting a little bored with being cooped up and decided to take a walk.

Judy enquired of the guard how long the train would be staying and she understood him to say 45 minutes. So we wandered off to see the town. When we were half way down the street we heard the train whistle behind us in the station.

"That's not our train is it Judy?" I fearfully enquired. "No" She answered. "He said 45 minutes"

"Are you sure it was not for 5 minutes!"

We both turned and sprinted back down the road only to see the last coach disappearing round the bend. Now in a blind panic we enquired if we could get a taxi and maybe catch the train further down.

In Rhodesia it was not uncommon, if one missed the train in Salisbury, to get in a car and join it at Norton a small station some thirty miles down the track.

"No hope" the Station Master informed us. "That was the boat train express".

Our hearts sank. Here we were only 36 hours from home and already we could see our trip ending in disaster. Would we really have to return home and confess that we were not yet mature enough to be allowed out on our own?

After making us sweat for a while the Station Master informed us

"The Johannesburg boat train will be passing through at 4 o'clock tomorrow morning and you can continue on that. "

He added with a smile "Don' t miss that one!"

He kindly phoned through and had our luggage taken off our train and we could collect it as we passed through DeAer, a town some distance away.

This settled, and with a great sigh of relief, we returned down the road to visit Kimberly. We now had about twelve hours to waste. Luckily we both had our handbags but were dressed for comfort in old slacks and sandals.

Not knowing the town at all, we thought that possibly we could get a bed for the night at the Convent. Having both gone to the Convent school in Salisbury we thought that maybe we had a toe in the door. But after ringing the front door we were told in no uncertain terms that the Nuns there did not accommodate waifs and strays.

We retired to an hotel and ordered a gin and orange each to drown our sorrows. I was well aware that a couple of Aunts of mine would be meeting the train that I was supposed to be on and I wondered how many panic buttons would be pushed when I didn't appear.

At a table near us were some young lads who looked presentable and we were soon part of a lively group. They stood us dinner and then took us dancing at some roof top dance hall. It must be admitted that this was much better than a bed in the Convent.

At 4 a.m. the next morning, after having had no sleep, we caught the train to Cape town. When we reached DeAr we were met by a very young policeman who took us to the luggage room and handed over our suitcases. That evening as we were sitting down to dinner a young woman stopped by our table and expressed surprise that we were on the train.

"I saw you being led away by the Police" she said. We didn't bother to explain and left her speculating as to what must have happened.

We arrived in Cape Town without further mishap but sadly in need of a hot bath. However there was no time now for such luxury.

Of course there were questions to be answered as my Aunts had telegraphed home when we did not appear on the scheduled train. We managed to parry these with an expertise neither of us knew we possessed. We caught the boat with about 4 hours to spare and were only too happy to escape from the endless queries as to how and where we had spent the 'lost hours' in Kimberly.

Being on board ship was a wonderful experience. The mail boats had a distinctive and unique scent that I have never found anywhere else. Although we were traveling in the lowly passenger class we found the cabin very comfortable although we didn't spend much time in it. There was so much to do, from deck games and swimming during the day to dancing the nights away. Being young and single we soon made a group of friends amongst whom was a young policeman who was going home before joining the Kenya Police. He was later killed by the Mau Mau. His name was Bert Selly.

Madeira, where the boat called after ten days at sea, was a very welcome break, and with several other youngsters we made the tourist trip around the wine bars tasting the wines and marveling at the hand made embroidery. It was a beautiful island and I made up my mind then to return some day, an ambition that I have not yet been able to realize.

We returned to the ship laden with bottles of the sweet, dark wine and that evening under a full moon we all sat on deck and drank them and sang. It was amazing how quickly the bottles emptied and before I knew it my stock for England had vanished.

The effect of the wine only became apparent when we staggered down the stairs to our cabin. Neither Judy nor I could stop laughing and the elderly lady who shared our cabin and had appointed herself chaperon had a hard time to settle us down.

But we paid for our hilarity the next morning as we both felt decidedly under the weather which the motion of the ship did nothing to dispel.

There was a very warm greeting for me in England from my sister Ann and her husband John, who I had not seen for several years. They now had a young son and had recently moved into their own home, in Oxford after having to share a house for several years. We spent many an evening reminiscing and I unloaded the gifts that the family had sent.

I made my base with them but traveled around as much as my limited funds would permit. Judy had independent finance and so she was able to get around more than I was.

The first time we left Oxford we decided to 'hitch' a lift to London. We had heard of other young people getting around this way and so thought we would try it. We stood on the roundabout outside Oxford and tossed a coin for who would be the first to 'hitch'. Judy lost and as a black car came in sight she closed her eyes and gave the traditional thumbs sign. Unfortunately the car was a hearse and the driver gravely pointed with his thumb over his shoulder, to the occupant in the back.

Once we had recovered from the giggles it was my turn to hitch and we succeeded in getting a lift to the outskirts of London in a very flashy red sports car. There we caught a train into the centre. The train was just leaving the station and we ran down the platform holding out suitcases and grabbed the first doors that we came to. Judy landed in the small engine room. I heard a thin voice calling through the wooden partition

"Roni where are you? I'm in some sort of driver's cabin." I rescued her at the next stop.

We really were 'country hicks' and should possibly never have been allowed out on our own!

As it was our first night in the big city we booked into an hotel, deposited our suitcases and then armed with maps and diagrams we proceeded to see the sites.

Judy was a picture of dismay when we came to Piccadilly Circus as she expected to see animals and acrobats. It also took several tries to persuade her to step onto an escalator. We were both disappointed in Buckingham palace as we expected something much bigger.

The next day, after we had recovered from paying the astronomical hotel account, we booked in to a small bed and breakfast. We went for a ride on the river braving the cold wind and rain and 'did' all the things that were expected of us, but we were both glad when, my allowance finished, we split up.

Judy went on an accompanied tour of Europe that had been paid for in Rhodesia, while I took a temporary clerical job in the university offices that did help finances somewhat.

Judy and I both went to watch the coronation but she had a seat on a stand outside the Cathedral while I stood in the rain all night at Hyde Park Corner. I was not to know that this was a famous pick up point and was amazed at the number of propositions that were put to me in so short a time.

It rained for most of the night and my sandwiches turned into a soggy mess. I was frightened to leave my place in the tightly packed crowd and stayed on my own wet patch of churned up mud, but I did see the parade.

When the Rhodesian troops came past the tears streamed down my face, as I shouted and cheered. I thought that they stole the whole show and I began to realize how homesick I was. The Rhodesian Coronation contingent was made up of picked men from the forces both black and white. They were all royally entertained while in England.

The story is told of a young white Officer of the Rhodesian Light Infantry being entertained at a very posh cocktail party.

"Do you have any black officers?" he was asked by Lady X.

"No, Mam", he replied. "Our officers are white but our privates are black".

"How fascinating!" She replied.

After a couple of months I plucked up the courage and went to Scotland to meet John's parents. They were a wonderful old couple and received me with open arms. I found the situation difficult as John and I had never become officially engaged. One reason was that he could never afford the ring!

Before going up to Scotland I went with Judy to visit Bert Selly's family in Devon. I think Bert would have very much liked to have developed his friendship with Judy but he was already committed to joining the Kenyan police. While walking over the cliffs I had been bitten by some insect on my hand. This festered and on arriving back in London I went into a chemist and asked for some 'muti' to put on it. The assistant looked at me blankly. It have never occurred to me that 'muti' was not an English word as we had always used it for ointment or medicine. I was advised to go to a doctor but there just wasn't the time as I had booked a sleeper on the train leaving for Scotland within an hour.

When I found my compartment I was cold and feeling rather unwell. As I was the only one there I turned up the heaters and settled down. Just as the train was leaving a lady rushed in.

"Hullo" she said. I'm from Skye. Isn't it hot in here!"

And she proceeded to turn off the heaters and opened the windows. I shivered the night away in my cotton blanket that was provided by British Rail.

As soon as I got to Auchtermuchty John's mum took me to the Doctor. I was not allowed to put my hand in water and I found this extremely embarrassing as Mum had to do my washing for me. Being a thoroughly modern miss my underclothes were just bits of nylon held together with lace.

"They fare cover you!" was her verdict expressed in a typical Scottish way.

I found it very difficult to understand their accent as I'm sure they must have mine but we got on very well. They were staunch Presbyterians but Mum arranged for me to get a lift to the Catholic Church on Sundays.

I then traveled up to Dunkeld and spent a lovely week in the Highlands with John's sister Margaret. I approached the subject of religion with her.

"Margaret" I said "How do your Mum and Dad feel about John marrying me and me being a Catholic?."

"O well " she answered "John is so stubborn he might even have married a darky!"

We are still the greatest of friends and when I needed help in later years she was the first to hold out her hand to me. However I did come to realize at the time how little these good people understood about conditions at home.

I had spent a long time in writing a letter to John describing the coronation and trying to express my emotions on that occasion. John returned my letter to me with the spelling mistakes underlined. I was really shocked and hurt and very very cross. Although I knew that I was not a good speller I reasoned that he had committed an act of extremely bad taste if not downright rudeness. I did not write to him again, although his letters arrived with monotonous regularity begging for an explanation of my silence. I thought that if he could not work out for himself why I was silent he must be really insensitive.

Because I now felt so unsure of my feelings for John, and being united with Judy again in Oxford, we decided to stay in England and to take another nursing course. Then Mary wired me and suggested that as John had had another bad year and as Mum was finding finances very difficult I should return home. My emotions were now a mass of guilt. How could I have been so awful to John when he was struggling so hard to make a life for both of us! Also how could I have totally disregarded Mum's need! No, I was now needed at home and there I would go.

So leaving Judy I booked my passage to return East Coast, on the Durban Castle. This journey would take six weeks. We would sail through the Mediterranean, calling at Gibraltar, Marseille, Genoa, Port Said, through the Canal, Red Sea and then down the cost of Africa. The boat stopped at all these ports for a day or two and I realized that I probably would never get another chance to visit these places. The trip would also give me time to get my emotions sorted out and help me to decide on my future.

On board was a very nice American priest called Tom who was going out to a mission in Uganda. We became great friends. I complained that the men on board were very stuffy and he advised me to wait until the hot weather! How right he was.

When we docked at Genoa, with some friends from the boat, I spent a day in the tiny port of Rapallo, and I delighted in again catching sight of tropical flowers like the red bougainvillea.

My homesickness returned with a vengeance.

47

As we sailed out of Genoa that night a group of Italian men gathered in the stern of the boat and sang Arivadeci Roma which was a new hit at the time. It was so sad to hear it sung in their beautiful harmony and I cried just with the beauty of it and the sadness that parting from one's loved ones brings.

The next morning while at sea, I donned my swimming suit and a new straw hat, that I had bought at a stall in Genoa, and lay on the deck to catch some sun. I removed the hat at one stage and laid it on the deck. To my horror hundreds of lice scampered away on all sides. The hat went overboard and I hurried down to the steward to get my cabin fumigated. On the way I met Father Tom and related the sorry tale to him. He found it a great joke, and the next day unbeknown to me he pinned a notice to my back. It said simply "Occupied"

I struck up a friendship with Jim, who was changing boats at Mombassa and then continuing to Australia. We became quite serious. All the conditions were there for a ship board romance, what with the sun, sea and at night dancing under the stars to romantic music. When we reached Mombassa Jim asked me to join him and we could motor down to Salisbury. I was sorely tempted as I would have loved to have done that trip but I could see my Mother's face if I did! Young ladies did not travel with young men alone in those days. I was also strangely reluctant to break our relationship but lacked the courage to take a step that might have changed my life. And so we said a rather soppy "Goodbye" in a dock side cafe. Jim sang to me and I, instead of appreciating his vocal efforts, was sorely embarrassed

On the morning that we were to arrive in Zanzibar, I was up before daylight and stood at the rails of the ship to watch the sunrise. Long before the island rose out of the pink and red sea the scent of cloves wafted towards me on the warm breeze, spicy and full of romance. The sky to the East was streaked by brilliant color which was reflected on the sea turning the crests of the waves in the ship's wake into colored candy floss. I watched the island rise out of the east as the red sun came up out of this painted sea. As we got nearer to land I could make out palm trees and the golden sands of a necklace of beaches. Once we disembarked I became enchanted with the narrow winding streets and the old Arab houses, protected by the most incredibly carved doors. The markets with their varied produce from fish to tropical fruits, materials of gauze and silks, bangles, beads and baubles enthralled me.

I sat at a wayside tavern and watched the inhabitants pass by. Arabs, Africans, Indians and an occasional European rubbed shoulders in the press of people. There was such a variety of skin color and dress fashion. The flowing white robes and colored fezzes of the Arab men accompanied by the dark, all embracing somber dress of their women. Bright Indian saris contrasted starkly with the near nakedness of the Africans.

I wandered around and finally came to the local hospital. I entered into its' cool corridors and walked along the shady verandas and thought,

"I could live on this island and work in this hospital"

And so I sought out the Matron's office with the intention of offering my services as a nurse. On learning that I was Rhodesian trained her manner became very stiff and she told me in no uncertain terms that I would not be welcome.

"All appointments were made through the Colonial Office in London" She told me. "You would have to return to England and apply from there, but I am not sure that we would recognize your training."

Now I was extremely proud of being a Rhodesian and objected strongly in being told that I was not "good enough".

And so when the ship sailed the following morning I was aboard her and my dream of living and working on a romantic island sank into the Indian ocean.

Within the decade Tanganyika won its independence from Britain and became Tanzania. Zanzibar was given to Tanzania and became another province of that country.

The Africans living on Zanzibar started a persecution of the Arabs and Indians living there. It began slowly and then suddenly one night the flames were fanned and rape and pillage swept the Island. The Arabs and Indians were killed in their hundreds and those fleeing by sea were mercilessly caught and drowned. For days bodies were washed ashore.

The beautifully carved doors and the Arab houses were burnt to the ground and the plantations of cloves destroyed.

Had I obtained work in Zanzibar would I have been repatriated in time to escape the slaughter? Or would my blood have joined that of countless others staining the waves that lazily washed the bright shore.

The boat docked at Biera and after a 24 hour train journey I returned to the bosom of my family. Mum cried when she saw me and the bone crushing hugs and kisses from John told me that I had made the right choice in returning to him.

I had only been home for a week when Jim appeared in Salisbury. He had made the trip down by truck. He begged me to marry him and go with him to Australia. It was all very embarrassing and difficult not to say tempting, but I remained firm and Jim continued on his way alone.

I wonder how my life would have been if I had gone with him.

Family finances were indeed very strained. Mary, with two young children was going through a divorce and Mum having given up the boarding house was living off a very meager pension. Because of the bad rains John's last tobacco crop was a failure and he returned to work in the butcher shop in Karoi. The owners of the farm he had been managing returned from abroad and took over the running of it.

And so I returned to work, this time in the Fever Hospital in Salisbury. During this year the country suffered an epidemic of polio. We were not prepared for such an emergency and were short of trained staff. We worked very long hours, and by today's standards our equipment was bulky and inefficient. The disease seemed to strike the young healthy men, many of them rugby players, whereas a few years previously it was a child's disease

The epidemic slowly subsided and John and I made plans to get married. Mum insisted on a formal wedding although I would have been content with a small informal gathering. Eventually we ended up with an invitation list of a couple of hundred, and so to cut the numbers we were married at 10a.m. on Monday, 9th. November.

CHAPTER 5

"O no!" I said as I opened my eyes on my wedding day "I've got a sty"

Sure enough when I staggered to the mirror and peered into it I could see the top lid of one eye, red and swollen. I knew from experience that within twenty–four hours the lid would produce an angry boil with a horrible yellow head. The eye would refuse to open in the morning and pain would shoot from it. What a way to start a honeymoon when I wanted to look seductive and alluring for my new husband.

Sties had been cropping up with monotonous regularity lately and I reasoned that it was because I had become rundown with all the extra duties that I had undertaken in the hospital over the last few weeks.

Although I had stuffed myself with extra vitamins and tonics they had not disappeared and were sometimes accompanied by boils on my back. I was not to know that these distressing eruptions were a sign of a more sinister malady within my body. Although subject to various pains at certain times of the month, I had disregarded them, and continued to work.

I quickly dressed in jeans and hurried to the hospital where I begged an injection of penicillin from the nurse on duty.

That done I could only hope that Mary would be able to disguise the offending eyelid with makeup and that the penicillin would halt the progress of the sty.

Returning to Mary's house, where I had spent the night and from where I would leave to go to the church, I surrendered myself to the administrations of my family. Judy and Mary would act as bridesmaid and matron of honor and of course my beloved Mum must have a place of honor in the proceedings. They all fussed around me bathing my eye, offering aspirin end eventually dressing me in the silk and lace dress that Mary had made for me. As Mary applied cosmetics to my face paying particular attention to the offending eyelid, I started to cry. The eye shadow ran down my cheeks making blue streaks on the artificial bloom of my cheeks. Really this was just too much!

"Now stop that" said Mary "or I wont finish your makeup".

I stopped! But my nerves still felt raw and I wished with all my heart that the day was over. I was not to know that there was worse to come.

As I didn't have a male relative that I could call on to give me away this duty was performed by an old family friend Malcombe, who had stayed at the Villa for many years and had watched me grow up.

John had become a Catholic. Not with any prompting from me. He took his new religion very seriously and read books on the lives of the Saints and the theory of Catholicism, whereas I wore it like an old comfortable glove. Our marriage was to be a Nuptial Mass celebrated by Father Seed who had received John into the church. He had also been a family friend for more years than I could remember and had given me my First Holy Communion so many years ago in Umtali, and had officiated at Dad's funeral.

During the rehearsal of the wedding ceremony a few days before the event, I stated that I was not going to promise to 'obey'. Honor I didn't mind but I felt that I could not guarantee the obey part for the rest of my life. This statement caused a greet deal of upset. Father Seed said that it was normal to obey one's husband and John was hurt. But the offending word was omitted from the ceremony.

Malcombe and I walked up the isle and I saw John waiting at the altar. By prearrangement Malcombe stopped at the bench where Mum was standing alone, and I turned to the left and gave her a hug and kiss. Mum was taken by surprise and I saw the tears start in her eyes. I turned around and walked up to the altar to stand beside my husband.

I had given John a missal for a wedding present and I was surprised to see him holding it in his hands, open at the wedding service. I heard Father Seed say in a harsh undertone,

"Put that away. You don't need it!"

I could not suppress a small giggle and was rewarded with a stern frown from Father Seed,

And so we were duly married.

The reception was held in a hall adjacent to the church and for a couple of hours we talked, danced and laughed with our guests. At last the time came for me to leave to get changed and I threw a garter for tradition. My bouquet of red roses I would put on Dad's grave later in the afternoon.

John had managed to purchase a very second hand Willis jeep. It was the first car that he had owned and it was his pride and joy. This car had a character all of its own and had it been human I would have awarded it a prize for being a first class male chauvinist pig. It hated me! I considered myself a very competent driver but I only had to get into it and she/he broke down. However, even John considered that it probably would not make it to Inyanga in the mountains of the Eastern Districts where we were to honeymoon. And so he had borrowed a car from a friend in Karoi to take us on honeymoon.

On leaving the reception it would not start and we had to be pushed by all the wedding guests. We stopped at Mary's house where I changed once again to a more comfortable dress and luckily discarded my high heeled shoes. John in the meantime removed the traditional Kipper from the engine the smell of which was already wafting into the cab, and then we set off.

It was the beginning of the rainy season and we were only halfway up the foothills when the car developed engine trouble. Now John might have been a good farmer or butcher but mechanic he was not! Well neither was I! After tinkering with the engine for some time John told me to get into the driver's seat and we would push start the car. But however I released the clutch it was never right, according to John, and so we changed places. I pushed and John took the wheel. This didn't work either but rather than give up we continued to struggle along.

Then the heavens opened and the dirt road became a muddy stream. The back wheels threw up a continual shower of red mud which slowly covered me and my new outfit. My feet slipped on the wet surface and I lost my shoes. I landed several times, face down on the road. My hair usually a dark blond clung to my head as a red cap.

At last a car appeared and the driver gave us a tow to the nearest hotel. We never did reach Trout Beck, the hotel where we had reservations and we certainly didn't give the impression of honeymooners, when we entered the reception area of the Rhodes Hotel, tired out and wet through. What was more we weren't talking!

The atmosphere didn't improve when all our spending money had to be laid out to get us back to Karoi, and repair the car in order to return it in a reasonable condition to it's owner.

More money troubles awaited us. Amongst the first post that we received on our arrival back in Karoi, was a tax demand for three years tax that John had neglected to return the forms for. And so all the money that we had received as presents went into the Government coffers! As this did not clear the debt I took a job working behind the counter at the local Farmers Co Op.

An official from the Vatican visited Salisbury in the early months of that year and there was to be great celebrations in the town. John and I returned to Salisbury for the event and joined a very large crowd who had gathered for an open air mass in the grounds of St. George's College. The seats for the lay congregation were arranged in a semicircle around the alter but there was a large space between it and the first row of seats. We were late arriving having come in from Karoi and stopped to change before going to the college. I wore my going away outfit which was a gold coat dress that I had made myself. Fashion in the 50s decreed that a stiffened petticoat be worn under the dress to give the skirt a flare. Under this, to protect your stockings from the harsh stiffening one wore an ordinary petticoat. With all these different layers around your waist it was difficult to feel if all was well.

Because we were late the only seats available were across the open space in front of the alter. We were directed to these chairs by an usher and told to hurry as mass was about to begin. As I started across what then seemed a vast expanse I felt the fastening on my stiff petticoat come loose. I made a hasty grab to my waist and said a quick prayer that it would hold until I had reached my seat, but it was not to be. The petticoat slipped further down my hips. I whispered to John and after one glance down at the offending, descending garment he hurried away from me, his head down and his face burning. The petticoat now almost around my ankles, I had no option but to step gracefully out of it, and retrieve it from the ground in front of that huge crowd. As it was stiff there was no way by which I could bundle it up into a small ball, and with the horrible thing waving like a flag over my arm I hurried after John and sank thankfully into my seat. I thought that I had handled the situation with dignity, and I must admit that seeing the funny side I couldn't stop giggling but John was mortified and refused to acknowledge me as I sat beside him.

Karoi was, at that time, a very small village that served an ever increasing farming community. Before the war it was only a spot on the road to the north, but when the men returned from the hostilities the Government opened up large tracts of the area and offered it as tobacco and maize farms to those men who had been on active service in the Rhodesian forces.

It boasted an hotel, the Farmers Co Op, two butcher shops and a couple of Indian bazaars. There was, however a fairly large African clinic staffed by African Orderlies and a resident doctor who also attended to the European population in a private surgery. If a European required hospitalization they would have to travel into Sinoa, some sixty miles south or else Salisbury which was 120 miles distant. At that time all Africans received free medical but Europeans paid for any services in this direction. However there was no opening for me as a nurse and so I began a new career as shop assistant.

John did not approve of this as he had always stated that his wife would not go out to work. However finances being as strained as they were, on this occasion he did not object but he did stipulate that it was only a temporary stop gap.

After living in the hotel for a few weeks, we managed to rent a small farm cottage within three miles of the village and set up home. As there was only one room we turned this into a sitting room come diner and we slept on the veranda which was screened in with wire gauze. We had hardly settled in when there was a very heavy thunder storm and the veranda roof proved to be no better than a sieve. We ended the night with John in the bath and me on the floor in the small passage!

We had been given two very small kittens, which we named Bali Ha'i and Tensing, and we both loved them dearly but I just could not get them house trained. We had an old couch and chairs inherited from John's bachelor days and one of the kittens chose the corner of the couch as a toilet. No amount of scrubbing could remove the pungent odor that rose from the cushion when one sat on it and no amount of pepper liberally strewn over the cushion stopped the kitten from making use of it.

To hide our embarrassment, whenever anyone came to visit us both John and I would make a dive to sit on the couch, in a vain effort to hide the smell. Our visitors obviously thought that we were very much in love and couldn't bear to be parted!

This was far from the truth as we both found it difficult to settle to married life and argued over the stupidest things. Had there been reliable transport at my disposal I would have packed my case and left several times.

On the one occasion that I did make it to the village lugging my baggage, I failed to get a lift into Salisbury, and having no money to pay for the hotel I had to return to the house.

A very humiliating experience!

John started work in the butchery at about 5a.m. Being a very new wife I considered it my duty to see that he went away on a full breakfast. As the stove in the cottage was an old wood one I would have to rise at 4a.m. to get the fire going. One morning as I struggled with the stubborn stove, I doubled over with pain in my abdomen. It was not long before I was vomiting my heart out and by the time John left for work I was running a slight temperature.

In the hope that I only had a slight food poisoning John left me but returned a couple of hours later. By this time I was in great pain and on the point of collapse. John bundled me up and we went to the Doctor's house. As I suspected the Doctor diagnosed an appendicitis and he advised a hurried departure for Salisbury.

After, what seemed a never ending journey in a borrowed car, we collected Mum, who had been informed by phone, of the situation and I was admitted into my old hospital.

After hurried consultations I was rushed to the theatre. The problem then became more apparent and not only was my appendix inflamed but I had been bleeding internally. Apparently this had been happening over several months and it was only when the hemorrhage became acute that the symptoms developed enough to make me ill.

This then was the cause of all the sties and boils that I had been suffering from and the feeling of debilitation that had plagued me for so long.

I was lucky to recover as soon as I did. This in part was due to Mum who nursed me when I was discharged from hospital.

During my convalescence, in Salisbury there was time for reflection and I came to realize if our marriage was to endure both John and I would need to change our attitudes.

I did understand that at 36 John was very set in his bachelor ways and I was inclined to be too independent. We discussed the situation with the result that I knuckled down and tried to ease the situation. John being of the old Scottish school never did change his idea that he was Lord and Master!

Ever ready to get back to farming, John accepted a position of farm manager on a farm called Shambatungwe and we moved house to a larger if not drier one.

During this year Mary and Mum often came to spend the odd weekend with us and Berry and Marrianne, Mary's children, spent a couple of weeks here.

We introduced Mary to Fred who was farming in the area and whom we had met at a social gathering at the local farmer's club. John and I both liked Fred but were of mixed feelings when they announced their engagement. It was a difficult situation as Mary was Catholic and had been married before. I suffered from a guilty conscious for having introduced them.

However, the damage had been done and I suppose if it had not been Fred it would have been someone else. Mary was a very attractive woman.

Fred had come up from South Africa at the end of the war and was buying a farm on the outskirts of Karoi. As he had not served in the Rhodesian forces he did not receive a free one, but he was an excellent farmer being an Afrikaner and was busy developing his land. Mary and Fred would have a hard time for the first few years but were happy to take the chance that had been offered to them.

John's jeep, never in the best of health, finally gave up the ghost and we were stranded seven (you had said earlier that it was 3 miles out of the village. What moved – you or the town?) miles from the village without any transport. John put it up for sale but was not swamped with offers. The first buyer looked it over and after tea offered a sum.

"How much do you think it will cost you to have it fixed?" John asked.

"O, I don't intend to fix it." Came the reply. "I want to convert it into a chicken house."

John couldn't allow his pride and joy to become a chicken house and refused the offer.

Eventually the mechanic from a local garage offered to take the jeep. He would repair it, he said and would then pay for it in installments.

"Wasn't I right to hang on for a decent offer?" John boasted.

Well the Jeep was repaired and was last seen disappearing in a cloud of dust towards the Bechuanaland border. We never did receive any money for it.

During this year we met and became friends with Nigel who worked for the Water Department and was responsible for looking after the reservoirs and boreholes in the Chirundu Valley. He was a terribly shy red–haired bachelor and he often took me with him when he went on a day trip to the valley. We went by four wheel drive Jeep over some of the roughest roads in Africa and I got my first sight of the Zambezi Valley. The soil for the most part was a sandy loam and supported Mapani scrub. The Africans living there were a very backward branch of the Tonga Tribe and still hunted with bows and arrows and spears.

The area that we visited was eventually to be flooded by the waters of the Kariba Dam but at that time the site had not been decided upon.

At site X which was below the Kariba gorge, lived a European family who were employed by the Government monitoring the flow of the Zambezi. They always made us very welcome and we usually had our salad lunch there. It was much too hot to eat any cooked meal. Their house was right on the banks of the river and I was amazed at the rate and height that the pawpaw trees grew to. It was no wonder that the Zambezi Valley around Chirundu became a huge sugar growing area. Later I was able to repay some of their kindness when their young son contacted malaria and was bought up to the high velt to regain his strength.

As we entered and left the valley the Jeep had to be sprayed to prevent the spread of Tsetse fly which was very prevalent.

In order to supplement the very low wages that John was paid as a farm manager I grew vegetables and kept chickens and ducks. I borrowed a bicycle from one of the farm laborers and took some vegetables into the village where my friends in the Co Op changed them for dry goods like sugar or flour. However John informed me

"You have no right to sell the produce as we didn't pay for the water and the ground is not ours"

I could not understand this reasoning but my weekly commercial ventures ceased. I was sure that if I had approached the owner of the farm he would have allowed me to sell these few vegetables but in case John would consider that I had 'gone over his head' and this cause another argument I allowed the matter to rest.

One day I extravagantly bought two kippers for our meal. It might not seem much nowadays but as a change from just vegetables or eggs it was a luxury. I laid them out on the kitchen table ready for cooking when John was ready to eat. They must not be overdone.

While my back was turned Bali Ha'i crept into kitchen and quick as a flash she took a kipper. I saw her out of the corner of my eye and immediately gave chase. She ran under the tractor parked at the back door and I crawled after her. She then made for a tree standing nearby and jumped up it. I was not far behind and grabbing her tail I extracted the fish. We both fell to the ground but I still held onto the kipper. Once back in the kitchen I washed it and cooked it for John's supper. I watched him eat it knowing that he had no idea of the drama that had taken place and smiling secretly to myself. What the eye does not see the stomach will tolerate!

The chickens and ducks had originally come from Mum but one night some wild animal, a stoat or weasel, got into the run and killed them all except one poor old duck called Josephine. She was badly hurt but I nursed her back to life. However she was very lonely and we were short of food so I'm afraid that she was destined for the pot.

I considered that at least I owed Nigel a dinner for all the trips that he had taken me on and I sent him a note asking him to come to dinner and that we were having Josephine. Nigel didn't turn up and John I eventually sat down to the meal by ourselves. It was only later that I discovered that Nigel's absence was due to the fact that he thought that Josephine was a girl friend of mine who would have been joining us for dinner!

When I arrived in Karoi the Catholic church was no more than a shack built of poles and grass. As one sat at mass one could watch the white ants climb up the walls. Eventually the Catholic farmers in the district clubbed together and a respectable church was built with a resident priest to serve not only the European congregation but the very large African community that was spread around the area. But in 1955 our community was served by a priest who came to the area once every three months. He was an elderly, dyspeptic man who served a very large area of several thousand square miles and was usually tired out by the time he reached us. When Father Carraman came to Karoi he would stay at the house of one of the European congregation in the hope that he would have a quiet night and a decent meal.

He chose our house one month because we had no children and therefore he should have been able to have some peace and quiet.

All went well to begin with. Supper was served and eaten and we all retired to bed early. As soon as the lights were out Bali Ha'i decided to steal something from the pantry and knocked over the pots and pans from the rickety shelf there. It took a little while to calm the priest and assure him that all was well and we were not being attacked by banshees.

The tobacco barns on our section of the farm were jerry built and in a very poor state of repair. The walls could not, by any stretch of the imagination be called straight.

When reaped the tobacco was tied to sticks that in turn were hung up on a wooden trellis fixed inside the barn walls. The barns were very tall and built in rows with about six adjoining each other. At the bottom of the barns were large metal pipes called flues that conducted the heat from the furnace at the back of the barn. At the start of the curing the tobacco was allowed to dry out and then the heat was increased until the leaves took on color and were cured. Thermometers were hung in the barn and a very strict watch was kept on the process which took about a week depending on the quality of the tobacco.

The night that Father Carraman stayed with us a stick of tobacco fell off the trellis and landed on the very hot flue. In no time the whole barn went up in flames.

We heard the crackle of the flames and the falling roof timbers and rushed out. John flew towards the barns and I struck the alarm as hard and as long as I could. This was an old plough disc that hung up on a tree and was struck with a metal bar each morning to summon the labor force to work.

The Africans came streaming out of the compound and a water chain was soon formed but despite all our efforts the fire spread to the adjoining barn aided by the wind. As this one went up with a terrible 'Whooshing' sound we then concentrated on saving the third barn on that row.

In the morning light we were able to assess the damage. Two barns and their contents utterly destroyed and the tobacco in the third barn ruined because of the water that had been poured on it.

Indeed as besides losing all the tobacco, both barns were then out of commission until they could be repaired and so we lost tobacco in the fields as there was no place to cure it and the crop must be reaped as it ripens. The fire couldn't have happened at a worse time.

But to crown it all Father Carraman never asked to stay in our house again. Poor man!

The Surgeon, who had operated on me earlier in the year had warned me that it was possible that we would be always childless but to my delight I fell pregnant. It was not an easy pregnancy and I suffered morning sickness from day one until the baby was born. I consumed Bicarbonate of soda by the pound to no avail, watched my diet, and did all that I could think of to alleviate the depressing symptoms. This John could not understand.

"Cows don't have morning sickness" (What about him saying cows deliver on all 4's so why can't you?) he informed me.

"Why should you?"

"It's all in the mind!" he added.

Due to the trouble that I had had the previous year our local doctor kept his eye on me and when I had reached seven months he insisted that I go to Salisbury to get expert care. John was in the middle of the tobacco season and could not afford the time to take me into town so we decided that I should have to get a lift.

Frightened and feeling very unsure of myself I packed my case and John took me into the village in a borrowed truck. He dropped me at the side of the main road and I was astounded to discover that he would not be staying with me while I was waiting for a complete stranger to come along and offer me a lift.

"I can't afford the time" He said, and added "Have you got a hat to wear while you wait?"

In retrospect I realize that I should have put my foot down and insisted that he stay but my stiff pride would not let me and I turned my back on him and walked away while he drove home.

I stayed with Mum while waiting the birth of my baby. During this time Mary and Fred were married and although Mum and I were not able to attend their wedding in the registry office I had decorated Mum's cottage with huge red poinsettias and they made a beautiful backdrop for their reception.

When I came into labor it was Mum who took me into hospital and after a normal delivery Lorelynn Jane was born. I thought she was the most wonderful baby in the world and cried my eyes out when I first held her. She became the centre of my universe.

I had left Karoi at the end of July and without telling me, in August, John had resigned from the farm and started a new job in Kariba in a butchery. There had been no bonus on the last tobacco crop as the owner said that there had been no profit. The pay of a farm manager was a mere pittance as housing, water and fuel were free. However if John had insisted on a written contract we might have been able to secure some money from the farm owner. The prospect of a good salary in Kariba, now that he had a daughter to support, did influence John. He thought the world of Lorelynn and was extremely proud of her. She was to remain his favorite, a fact that he did not hide from the other children when they arrived.

Our baby was baptized, Lorelynn Jane after both our mothers as soon as I came out of hospital.

CHAPTER 6

The great Zambezi river rises in the very North Western corner of Zambia, almost on the border with Angola and Katanga and begins its' 1,650 mile journey to the Indian Ocean draining an area of some 465000 square miles on it's way. In its' middle and lower reaches and over millions of years the great river has carved out a valley that varies in width from ten to twenty miles. The sides of this valley rise up on either side in foot hills that then rise to an impressive escarpment that finally levels off 2000 – 3000 feet above the river.

Forming the border between Zambia and Zimbabwe, the Zambezi plunges over the Victoria Falls, so named by David Livingstone but more picturesquely called Mosi–Oa–Tunya (The Smoke That Thunders) by the African people. These magnificent falls are 350 feet high and are the result of a prehistoric earthquake.

Below these falls and more or less in the middle of the valley this great river runs between a series of deep gorges and areas where it flattens out to a mile wide deceptively peaceful flow.

There are many places that could have been made into great dams and in 1955 the Government of the Federation of Rhodesia and Nyasaland, (as Zimbabwe, Zambia and Nyasaland were known at that time) decided to construct a hydroelectric project at a gorge called Kariba. When completed the waters that had been dammed up would cover an area of 2000 square miles and create a lake 175 miles long.

Several different sites had been examined for this dam and a great deal of time and money were expended in the preliminary explorations. The river flow at all seasons had to be monitored, rock samples examined and gorges explored.

The roads into the area were rough tracks only negotiated by four wheel drive vehicles. There was no cleared areas for aeroplanes to land on in the thick bush. An all weather road access into the valley to Kariba, became of the highest priority.

Karoi being the closest village at a distance of 120 miles suddenly found itself in the front line of the development although the railway line from Salisbury, ended some sixty miles away to the south at a little siding called Lion's Den.

The Great North Road, from Salisbury to Lusaka and the north, crossed the Zambezi at Chirundu which was much further east than the dam site and as such could not be used as an access down the escarpment.

After many months surveying, it became clear that the easiest and least expensive route down the mountains was one that had been used by elephants for centuries on their yearly migration.

So from the top of the escarpment a road was laboriously constructed, branching off from The Great North Road at Mkuti, a very small village, at the start of an elephant path.

As the building of the road progressed different places took the names of events that had happened there. When relating one's recent journey over it one would say

"As we approached cobra corner" or "Coming around baboon ridge" Perhaps it would be "As we passed leopards leap"

All this added to a descriptive narrative as no trip over this half completed road was without incident.

It is one of the most picturesque end exciting roads that I have ever driven over. In most places the mountain wall stretches up on one side covered with thick forest, and a sheer cliff descends into the depth of a valley on the other. Huge boulders line the road as it twists and turns, and rises and descends on it's downward way. And always when crossing the crest of a hill, the main valley floor stretches away into the blue distance. Because the road had been carved out of the mountains, land slides were quite common especially in the rains. At these times one just had to wait until the road was cleared which could at times, take several hours.

At night as you came around a bend and entered a dip in the road, the headlamps of the car would suddenly pick out the white trunks of ghost trees that grow in the damp of a crevice in the hills. In these clefts, during the rains, there was often a stream meandering down or descending as a waterfall from a hidden spring higher up.

Monkeys and baboons watched with solemn eyes when the cars or lorries passed then swung away to disappear in the thick bush.

Within a few months another access road on the Zambian side was constructed so that the building of the dam went ahead from both sides of the river.

A swing bridge had been strung over the river but I never summoned enough courage to cross it, a fact I greatly regret now. To me the swirling waters of the Zambezi were very frightening.

In the valley, amongst the first and most pressing problems to be faced by the Government was the removal and resettlement of the people of the Tonga tribe who had lived there for many generations. Their villages and lands would eventually be covered by the waters of the dam. More important to these people, the burial grounds of their ancestors would be swept away. The Tonga's worshipped their dead together with other Gods. The moving of the tribes became a political problem and proved to be a very difficult task. The Africans believed in a river God called Nyaminyami who would not allow the damming of the river and therefore it was not necessary for them to move. This being the case it was obvious that the Europeans were persecuting them. They refused to move and eventually as the waters of the dam rose they had to be forcibly taken to the modern brick villages on the escarpment that had been built for them.

The Ngangas and Witch Doctors predicted grave consequences if the construction of the dam went ahead and that Nyaminyami would demand human sacrifice.

Besides this human problem there remained that of the animals that wandered freely through the valley.

Elephants can swim but there were numerous varieties of antelope, monkeys, baboons, bush pigs and snakes (to mention a few) that would drown when the waters rose or if caught on an island, would slowly starve to death. In the early days of the construction efforts were made to herd the animals out of the area. But these proved unsuccessful and as the waters rose and islands appeared many animals were trapped there. An exercise called Noah's Ark led by an Intrepid European from the Government Game Department was put into operation. The animals were cornered, if necessary tranquillized, and removed by an armada of small boats to higher ground. This was often a very dangerous exercise but there was no lack of young blades both black and white who looked forward to the excitement of the chase and the love of the wild animals. Not least was the lure of the freedom of the life that a game ranger lives.

The Zambezi valley was also a tsetse fly area. The fly which carries the dreaded sleeping sickness is a pest to humans and animals and lives in the dense bush of the lowland areas. A prolonged and expensive campaign to rid the area of this pest was undertaken. All vehicles entering or leaving the area had to be sprayed with insecticide in large sheds and aerial spraying continued for many months.

Happily at the same time the malaria mosquito was eradicated from the immediate area of the dam construction, but the loss of other benign insect life must have been immense.

Because of the intense heat on the valley floor, accommodation for the personnel, who were to be employed on the construction of the dam and those in the service industries, was built on the hill sides to catch any breeze that might be in the area. The land was bulldozed out of the rock face to make a level area for these houses. Included in the development was a modern hospital and all the utility buildings that were needed by a community of several thousand people. The actual contract for the building of the dam was awarded to an Italian company and eventually several hundred Italians and their families were transported in.

However, when John agreed to open a butchery in Kariba there were few buildings and he started the business in a prefab hut on the valley floor. The heat there was almost tangible and although the shop was provided with an air conditioning unit it did not seem to give any relief. Meat was delivered twice a week by refrigerated railway lorry and stored in a large cold room at the back of the shop. Any disruption to the electricity supply and the meat went off within a couple of hours.

Obviously the first houses to be constructed were not for those people in the commercial section and although John was able to find room in a male mess there was no accommodation for Lore and I. We remained in Salisbury with Mum. We did however manage a couple of weekends in Kariba and on these occasions we flew up in a small piper club plane. The airstrip was, at fist, just an area of cleared bush, where the ant hills had been flattened, it was a few miles from the township and the pilot had to circle several times to ensure that there were no elephants or other game wandering over the strip, before descending

Eventually John managed to secure a house and we moved into Kariba when Lore was about four months old. John worked extremely long hours and when he came home he was exhausted with the heat. There were no other women within walking distance of our house and lacking transport I found the days rather long and lonely.

But Kariba did have its' compensations. Before the Italians arrived Kariba attracted the flotsam of a construction community and the characters were extremely varied and often colorful if not actually criminal

Laurie was a Canadian, in his fifties, who had left his wife and family behind when he had to beat a hasty retreat out of Canada, one step in front of the law. What his crime had been I never knew. He was lonely and missed his children. Every evening at about 5.30 he would appear at our front door and carry Lore off to the pub.

"Where is my Grand daughter?" he would call.

Lore would "Coo" at the sight of him and lift her arms in anticipation. Then the two of them would trundle down the hill side to the pub where for a short time Lore reigned supreme.

She was given her own glass with a spoonful of beer, and sat happily for the next hour holding court. She was then returned to me in time for bed before the heavy drinking in the pub commenced.

Tony was a young brother of one of the girls I had nursed with. He was employed by the telephone company and was busy laying cables. He was great fun and had a wealth of stories that kept me amused for hours. Unfortunately Tony enjoyed a party a little too much and spent most Saturday nights in one of the ditches that he had dug for the cables. On Sunday morning he would extract himself from the mud and come to our house begging a shower and Alka-Seltzer.

One day Tony borrowed a small boat and together we went for a trip down the Sanyarty river. This was before the waters had been dammed up and most of the gorge on this river flooded. It was a wonderful day. Lore was with a friend and I felt as free as a bird.

Because of the heat and humidity of the valley the vegetation was lush. The sheer rock sides of the gorge were covered with ferns and orchids, watered by streamlets that trickled down. Baboons barked at us as we went past them disturbed by the gentle chug chug of the outboard motor and fish jumped out of the water, their silver scales catching the sunlight that filtered down. Weaver birds fluttered and twittered around their colonies of nests that hung from the trees leaning out over the water. The call of the fish eagle floated over the still air. As we came to a sand bank I watched a crocodile slip silently into the stream without a splash or causing any ripples, a timely reminder not to swim in these waters. The long lazy day ended with a magnificent sunset in which the sky was colored with the reds and oranges so typical to the brief African twilight. All this beauty was to be lost under the rising waters of the great dam and I felt very sad but privileged to be one of the last people to ever see it.

A swimming bath was built at the very top of one of the hills. We all watched its progress with great interest in the hope that it would help us escape from some of the continuous, oppressive heat. One particularly hot night when we were unable to sleep because of the heat, John and I, with Lore in the back seat, drove up the hill in the vain hope of finding a cooling breeze. When we came to the half finished pool we found that it was full of water. The night was starlit and still. The water glistened and beckoned. Who could resist it? Lore remained asleep on the car seat. John and I stripped, jumped over the half fence and plunged into the pool. It was wonderful. Because the surrounding heat was so high the contrasting temperature of the water was invigorating and soothing and we swam around for a good half hour keeping our ears open for any sound from Lore in the car. We finally pulled ourselves out and sat on the side of the pool to regain our breath.

"What on earth is that black streak on your cheek?" I asked John thinking that he had been hurt.

He rubbed his face and his hand came away black. It was impossible to see what had caused it. He peered at me.

"Your hair is all black" He said. "And you have it all over your bottom".

On closer inspection we discovered that we both had black streaks all over our bodies. We donned our cloths and hurried home to the light. We were covered in tar! After some surreptitious enquiries, we discovered that in order to find out if there were any leaks in the pool the builders had filled it with water without cleaning the tar off the joints. This tar had of course floated to the top of the water and we had obligingly cleaned most of it off the surface with our bodies. We spent most of the rest of the night trying to clean it off with butter, but it was several days before the last remnants finally disappeared.

I became very familiar with 'The Elephant Path' during several trips back to Karoi. Mary had become pregnant and gave birth to twins which were very premature. Unfortunately one was already dead but Mary Lou survived although she was only 1lb 9oz. The babies were born in Sinoia and although Mary was allowed back to the farm, Mary Lou remained in the hospital for a couple of months. This meant that Mary had to make the 60 mile journey every day with her milk for the baby. As Barry and Marrianne had to be taken into the village school every day the family were rather stretched and so I journeyed in several times to give them a helping hand. Lore was already walking and the change from the heat of the valley was very welcome to us both.

The long Zambezi is subject to yearly flooding. The heavy rains to the far north, which fall in the early months of the year, take until August or September to reach Kariba, and then come down in a great surge of water. The dam across the river was built in a series of polder dams. The water was diverted to one side and a temporary enclosure built so that part of the the actual dam wall was constructed inside this temporary enclosure.

Due to a miscalculation or the early surging of the river this first polder dam was flooded before it could be properly completed and evacuated. Nyaminyami claimed His first sacrifice of three lives in this catastrophe as well as bulldozers and equipment that were swept away. The bodies were never recovered. As news of the catastrophe spread like a bush fire through the village, everyone made their way to the high banks and we stood in silence as we watched the still rising, turgid torrents sweep below us carrying logs and debris in its mad rush to the sea. On the highest point on the banks the local nganga stood in silence. Eventually a remembrance service was held and wreaths were thrown into the waters. There was nothing else that anyone could do. Nyaminyami was to claim 17 lives in all before the the construction of the dam was completed. However most of these tragedies occurred after we had left.

73

One Sunday we went to lunch with Peter and Jean. Peter was an engineer and had been recruited in England to work on the immense tunnel that went through the surrounding rock face and would house the mighty turbines to generate electricity. Jean his wife and two children had also come out. Jean was pregnant and maybe because of the heat was having trouble carrying the baby. The local doctor advised that she should be under the care of a gynecologist in Salisbury. Mum, ever ready to help anyone, had agreed to look after Jean and she took up residence with Mum until she was admitted into hospital. Eventually Jean's baby was safely delivered. I cared for the two older children while their mother was away.

Today we were celebrating the return of Jean and the new addition to the family. Just as lunch was finishing John rose unsteadily from the table.

"Ron" he said "I feel awful"

With that and before I could go to him he collapsed and fell to the floor. He was unconscious but breathing. My heart flipped over. He looked so dreadful lying there. His skin was grey and clammy, his pulse erratic. With Peter's help I made him comfortable on the floor and I knelt at his side while Peter called the local Doctor. We were so lucky to have one in the near vicinity. By the time the Doctor arrived John had regained conscious but I could see that he was very ill.

"I'm afraid that John has had a heart attack" the Doctor advised me. "He must get into Salisbury to a specialist as soon as possible".

And so we flew back to town to Mum and John was admitted to hospital. After extensive tests it was discovered that John's heart had been damaged by poison from his tonsils and they were removed, a very painful operation for a man of his age.

After a period for recuperation we returned to Kariba, but things were not the same. John and the owner of the business did not agree on many major policies and there were several arguments. John did not take these arguments lightly and would bring his bad temper and worries home with him. He refused to talk them over with me. I knew that there was something terribly wrong but did not know the cause. He became very difficult to live with as nothing I did was ever right. Eventually, John was fired and the whole sorry story came to light. It was something of a relief as I now knew that John's bad temper was not of my making and that he was not still ill as in my worry I had feared.

However, all was not gloom as while he had been in Kariba John had been offered a job in Lusaka which was in Northern Rhodesia. We packed up the house in Kariba and said goodbye to all our friends there. After a short period in Salisbury, during which time Lore turned one year old, we packed the car we had managed to buy and set out for Lusaka.

CHAPTER 7

The Central African colonies of Northern and Southern Rhodesia and Nyasaland had been formed into a Federation in 1954. This political move was not favored but imposed by the British Government as an economic cure–all for the area. Salisbury, being the biggest city, became the capital of the Federation and as such received the lion's share of the revenue. To the people of Northern Rhodesia and Nyasaland it seemed that Southern Rhodesia definitely got the better part of the deal and Salisbury earned the name of 'Bomber Zonky' which meant grab it all. There was no doubt that the wealth of the copper mines in the north of Northern Rhodesia was a great temptation to the somewhat impoverished Southern state.

When we arrived in Lusaka in November 1957, we were amazed to discover that the capital of Northern Rhodesia did not even have a tarred main road in the centre of the town. This road was called Cairo road and was a part of Rhode's dream of a Cape to Cairo highway. Eventually it would of course be surfaced and a very beautiful road it became with trees gracing the island in the middle.

John's new employer had arranged for us to live in a house that he owned, which was just outside the town. It was a very old house and was surrounded by tall gum trees that creaked and groaned whenever the wind blew. The house was enclosed by a gauzed veranda but had stood vacant for a long time. Water was provided from a well in the back yard which had an electric pump and the loo was down the back garden path. It was very different from the new modern house that we had had in Kariba.

It took several weeks for our furniture to arrive from Kariba and in the meantime we lived on empty paraffin boxes. We had managed to borrow a single bed but after one hot night of trying to fit two adults into it, Lore and I slept on the floor. This was fine except that there was a colony of hunting spiders who objected to having their sole occupancy of the house disturbed, and spent their nights scampering over our mattresses. I discovered that a spider's feet as they run over your face are extremely cold. Hunting spiders are very large and hairy, sometimes having a leg span of four inches. They look horrible.

"These spiders are giving me nightmares", I complained to John.

"Don't be silly Roni" He answered "You know they don't bite and they have been proved to be nonpoisonous" He added. "Besides they eat the mosquitoes".

This made the spiders no more attractive and I spent longer each night making sure that Lore's net was tucked securely into her mattress. It was alright for John. He slept in the security of the only bed.

Once more our finances took a downward curve due to a drop in John's salary. John had always kept a tight hold on the purse strings and had always insisted that "his wife" would never work. But for all that he was very tardy in paying the bills. After several final demands had arrived at our address I took over the domestic accounts to see that everything was paid on time. However all the checks had to be signed by him and if I ever wanted to purchase anything I had to take a signed check with me. This really annoyed me and hurt my already dented and bruised ego but as I did not contribute to the family finances I was unable to change the system. I could not get used to being 'The little woman who stayed at home with the baby'. I was not much use at talking baby talk all day and felt that I needed some mental stimulation. Moreover however much I tried our income was not covering our expenditure and I decided that I would have to take matters in hand.

I realized that nursing was out for me as John worked incredibly long hours and the staggered times of the nurses shifts would not be suitable with a young child. I knew nobody in Lusaka whom I could ask about work and had absolutely no connections in the business world. And so without informing my husband, who would I was sure strongly object, I dressed in my smartest clothes and with Lore in the pushchair I walked down Cairo Road, stopping at each shop to enquire if they had any vacancies. I first tried the chemist shops thinking that my nursing would give me an edge but to no avail. Then I entered the shops, requested to see the Manager and more or less pleaded for work. This to me was humiliating until one bright manager suggested

"Why don't you try the Government Employment Agency?"

I hadn't known that they existed! By the time I returned home that evening I had a job as a clerk in the Mechanical Workshops starting the following month. The last hurdle of informing John, I took that night as I handed him that month's accounts. With the evidence before him he could hardly object.

Life is so much easier when you know the ropes!

At the same time the well in the garden from which we drew our water was declared unfit for human consumption and we were moved into a flat on one of the back roads of the town. This flat was also owned by John's employer and the rent, as before, would be part of John's salary. It was not a residence to write home about as it had no garden but it was within walking distance of the crèche that I booked Lore into. I would be able to push Lore to it arriving as the doors opened and then sprint up the road to be in time for my work.

Lore and I both settled into our new life and although John was still not happy that his wife had shown a streak of independence he took the view that if it didn't upset his routine, he was pleased with the improved bank balance on our now joint account. There were no more final demands delivered to our address.

As we were both now earning money, we decided to invest in some land. We bought twenty acres on the outskirts of Lusaka, to be paid for over the next five years. There was nothing on the land but we could dream of one day building our dream house. The only thing that we did to that piece of ground was to bury John's old cocker spaniel, Pooch, on it. She was a black bitch and at the age of 15 had died quietly one night while on John's bed. She had been a great friend to him and we both mourned her passing. We did in time buy a golden spaniel who we called Misty. Misty was unfortunately run over but she had produced our next pet who we called Foggy. Spaniels were ideal for us as they are playful but very gentle with young children. At the same time we always had a cat or two in the family.

We slowly collected a group of friends. One family in particular we met through Lore, who had taken up with a little girl called Gail at the crèche. Her father Gerry was a policeman, and her mother Pat and I became very close friends. They were later to prove how strong their friendship was.

However the political situation in the country was not easy. African Nationalism was coming into its own and causing unrest in the country.

One night we were woken up by the sound of explosions. Both John and I ran out to the porch and watched in horror as a crowd of Africans, some fifty or sixty strong, marched down the road towards us shouting political slogans and chanting.

As they advanced they started to throw petrol bombs into the Indian shops on both sides of the street. There was nothing that we could do. We were hemmed in on both sides by the now screaming mobs. I'm afraid we spent the time cowering and sweating in fear behind the parapet and keeping our heads down only raising them to peer over the edge. My baby was asleep in the back room of the flat, and although feeling a deep pity and alarm for the Indians I was concentrating on not drawing the attention of the mob to our darkened flat. In truth I don't think my paralyzed limbs would have responded to any commands to move.

As the Indians, who lived on the top floors of their shops ran out of the buildings, they were set upon by the rioters. It was a horrific sight. Against the orange flames that were consuming the buildings, the black silhouettes of the rioters danced in a devil's reel. They were mad with power and alcohol and were looting what had escaped from the inferno in the shops. Above the roaring of the flames and the shouting of the Africans could be heard the screams of the Indians. The Africans even attacked the screaming children who were running around bewildered and frightened. In the light of the street lamps I saw Mr. Choudri, who always greeted me as I passed his shop on my way to the crèche, go down under an assault by three or four Africans. His wife ran to help him and was hit over her head. She fell under the feet of her attackers. Nadia their little girl not much older than Lore stood screaming in the doorway of their burning shop.

Although it seemed to continue for a very long time, in reality it was not more than half an hour before the police and fire engines arrived. We suddenly found that we could move and as our limbs obeyed our commands once more, we rushed out into the street to render what help that we could to the victims. I ran straight to Nadia and picked up the near hysterical child in my arms. I then put her in the safety of our porch while I returned to give first aid where I could, bandaging up the ghastly gashes that had been the result of slashes with machetes. Mr. Choudri had suffered a near mortal slash across his shoulder, that fortunately had missed any vital arteries as well as several smaller cuts. Fortunately his wife had no visible wounds but would possibly suffer from concussion. They had escaped death as the mob was so impatient to loot the shop. Some of the wounds would take weeks to heal but there were no deaths at that time. Perhaps the temptation of looting saved the Indians from more serious injury. Eventually the injured were taken away to hospital and the homeless were absorbed into the Indian community. Nadia handed over to a relative, when her parents were taken away by the ambulance.

The next day several friends from the crèche and work collected and distributed clothes and household goods to the Asians. Life seemed to settle down for a while. But the seeds of distrust between the races were now firmly sown.

Gerry against orders, told us that we should move house as we were too near the African locations and the area had been declared 'at risk'.

After much thought we approached John's employer and stated that we wished to move to a house that we considered would be safer. He reluctantly agreed and I started to house hunt. The fact that I was pregnant again was, at the time, both a blessing and an inconvenience. I had only really just settled into my work and had been given a promotion to Staff Clerk. I was disappointed that it seemed I would have to give up my job. Although John viewed my work with a supercilious smirk, I was extremely proud that I had proved that I could turn my hand to a clerical post. On the other hand Lore was now nearly three and if she was not to be an only child a sibling would have to be provided. Although not planned this seemed as good a time as any for another baby.

I discovered that as I had joined the British Civil Service I was entitled to those conditions of service that applied to officers recruited in Britain. When an officer had completed a tour of two years he or she was entitled to 4 months leave. If the tour had continued for three years the leave entitlement was six months. After careful calculations I worked out that in order to get my four months leave I would have to work until the baby was due, take two weeks occasional leave, work another months and then I would be at home with the baby for four months.

And so we once again moved house. This time it was a bigger house and had a garden. When we arrived there was a flock of pigeons in residence and Lore christened it "The House of the Doves".

Mary, in the meantime had produced a son, Mark. This time there had been no complications and both she and the baby were doing well. Fred persuaded Mum to give up her house in Salisbury and she went to live on the farm in a small cottage there. Mum often came up north to stay with us for short periods and she agreed to come up when our baby was due. And so the stage was set, or so it seemed.

John had joined a church organization St. Vincent de Paul, and spent most of his spare time helping the poor or at the church. It was a very worthwhile organization, but I'm afraid I resented the time that he spent there instead of helping me with Lore. After a long day at work and having to walk to and from it after collecting Lore, in the evenings I was exhausted. John of course went to work in the car as he began at 5.a.m. To complain would be useless as I was sure that he would just tell me to give up work regardless of the extra finance.

Mum arrived in Lusaka in good time for the birth of my baby and so I was relieved of the long walk to the crèche for about a week. However, labor started one afternoon at work and I walked home, to await developments. I had phoned John at his work before I left to tell him that I was in labor.

"I can't possibly leave the shop" he said.

"O, and by the way I have a meeting of St. Vincent de Paul after work" he added. "I'll be home as soon as I can after it is finished"

It was my stupid pride that stopped me from demanding that he come to fetch me.

By ten o'clock that night I was getting fairly desperate and John had not returned home. There was no telephone and John had the car and so I was forced to call on a neighbor to take me into the hospital. Mum remained at home to look after Lore.

Debra Ruth was born the following afternoon on 17th February 1960, after a very long and painful labor and I was badly torn. The repair was not carried out correctly and was to be the cause of complications later. However, Debra was perfect and entered the world crying her heart out. This she continued to do for the next six months.

Mum stayed with us while I went back to work for the extra month and we both battled with this child that just would not settle. The fact that Lore had been the perfect baby, who slept when required, walked, talked, and came out of nappies very early, I had put down to careful training. Debra changed all my ideas, and there were even times when the only way I could settle her was with a teaspoon of brandy. Unfortunately Mum, my ally and my prop, had to return to the farm when I started my long leave. I always hated her going.

To add to my troubles, Lore, my perfect child, started to display serious jealousy and at one time pushed Debra, pram and all, off the veranda where the baby was sleeping. Fortunately Debby suffered no ill effects.

To my earnest questioning she replied.

"We don't need Debby, and she cries all the time". I realized that I would have to spend extra time with Lore and involve her more in looking after her sister.

The Belgian Congo, then called Zaire, shared a common border with Northern Rhodesia, now Zambia, in the north. The Belgians suddenly decided to grant independence to their colony within six months in 1960. There had been no time for a systematic release of power. Within 5 days of independence the black Congolese army revolted against their white officers many of whom were killed. Some officers managed to escape and made a hasty exit from the Congo. The country disintegrated into chaos. The remaining Europeans panicked at the sudden emergence of the several armed African political parties, and fled the country by whatever manner that they could. Many came down to the Copper Belt from the wealthy provenance of Katanga and ran a gauntlet of armed gangs on the road. They were received by hurriedly organized charity groups as they crossed the border into Northern Rhodesia and were fed and clothed. Most had just left their homes with what they could pack into their cars and many were relieved of these goods at gunpoint by the marauding Africans.

Several stories trickled through of young girls being removed at gun point from the cars and never being seen again. One can only assume that if the rumors were true the fate of these youngsters was too terrible to contemplate. Certainly the murder and rape of several missionary nuns was verified. There was nothing that we, sitting comfortably and safely in our homes, could do to help except pray and help those that managed to cross the border. There was no army stationed in our country and the police were stretched to their limit dealing with the local African unrest, much of which we were ignorant of.

As the Congo sank further into mayhem with African killing African and no system of government, there was no method by which people could be traced. The United Nations were finally called in to restore order but proved to be quite ineffectual but a fragile peace was restored in 1964, after which the United nations withdrew their troops.

Within a few months war broke out again as various provinces tried to succeed from the central government. The opposing armies now recruited foreign mercenaries and no mercy was shown by either side. As is always the case it was the women and children who suffered the worst.

All this continual unrest on our northern borders, had of course a very unsettling effect on the European and Asian communities but life continued much as it had done in the past due in part to heavy censorship of the media. Not least was the feeling that "It couldn't happen to us".

The St. Vincent de Paul society were asked by the Social Services to find a home for a young girl who had been taken into care and sent down south to a secure hostel. Apparently her father had been selling her out as a prostitute to his business associates. The family was now suing the Social Services and bidding to have her returned. In order to attend court she had to be housed in a neutral home. John volunteered our home without consulting me, although I would be the one who had to care for her.

She stayed with us during the court case with very little disruption to our lives. The case was concluded and the girl, as a result of the verdict, was returned to her parents.

The Social Services then approached me with the surprising offer of a position looking after one of their homes in Ndola. This home was designed to be run as an ordinary family, where the father would go out to work and I, the mother, would look after the inmates. The 'father' would be on hand to help in the evenings. The home would house youngsters from the age of seven to seventeen who had committed some crime but were not material for a reformatory.

I had had no training in dealing with problem children and I refused with thanks, much to John's disappointment. I wanted to continue in my old job that was being held open for me. I was well aware that John was not happy in his work but was shocked when one evening I went to fetch him from the butchery.

"Ron", he greeted me. "I've handed in my notice and I leave here at the end of the month. You'll have to take that job in Ndola".

What could I say! I was furious. No amount of arguing would alter his decision. I wondered what had happened to his lofty ideas that his wife would never work!

So the next morning found me at the offices of the Social Services.

Certainly this position would solve the problem of having to put Debra into a crèche as I could have her with me, I would also still be a Civil Servant and as such my entitlement to their conditions of service would remain.

And so once again the family was on the move, this time to the north of the country on the Copper Belt just a few hours drive from the border of the Congo where a bloody civil war was raging with no end in sight.

I think that it was at this time that I began to realize that I was married to a dreamer. To John the grass would always be greener on the other side of the fence. Perhaps it was the fence that he could not tolerate. He could have found other employment in Lusaka but once again fate had played into his hands with the Social Welfare offer.

It was just before we left Lusaka that Joel came into our lives. I had of course had African servants before but Joel was someone special. He came originally from Nyasaland, now Malawi, and was an elderly man with a wife and a grown up family. He was an excellent cook and I came to trust him implicitly. Over the years that he and his wife Alice, were with us we became more friends than employer and employee. Debra was only a month or two old and I did not have a servant. I had decided to do without one while I was at home with her. The last servant had left under a cloud with half my linen as well as several items that we only discovered missing in the ensuing days.

Joel appeared one morning at our back door, with his cranky old bicycle and asked for work.

I replied "I'm sorry but I don't have work for you".

The next morning at sun up Joel was at the back door again with a big grin splitting his black face. There he stayed until I agreed to take him on. Not least in his favor was the fact that Lore walked right up to him and took his hand. The two then proceeded to have a long conversation half in broken English and half in Shona. By the end of the day Joel and his wife Alice had settled into the servant's quarters at the back of the house.

CHAPTER 8

Ndola was the centre of the rich copper mining belt in the north of Zambia. Although not a mining town in itself it was the administrative centre and did have a copper refinery. The nearby towns of Kitwe, Luanshya, Mufulira and Chingola had grown up around the mines owned by the Anglo American Mining Company and owed their development to this Company. Miners both black and white were housed in the Company's houses and educational, health and recreational facilities were also provided by 'The Big Boss'.

Conditions of service in the Company were very good and a fairly affluent society emerged with the usual ills and problems. Under the law for Europeans, as it was then, a child was deemed capable of committing a crime from the age of seven and could not be imprisoned until after 17. Depending on the gravity of the crime children were removed from their homes and either placed in a reformatory (of which there were none in Zambia the nearest being Salisbury) or housed in other 'safe houses'. There were institutions for those children from broken homes but it was considered unwise to mix the two categories. And so I was to start a home for children who had committed some crime or had proved to be too difficult to house in an ordinary institution but were not corrupt enough to be sent to a reformatory

After giving the situation serious consideration I came to the conclusion (on my own) that as most of the prospective inmates of my home would possibly have a history of domestic violence or some other unfortunate occupancy, what they required most was love. I had had no training and certainly was no psychologist and really was like a lamb led to the slaughter.

The Homestead as our house, was called was a large one situated in one of the quiet avenues in Ndola and was to draw its' inmates from the whole Copper Belt. The ordinary house had been added to and now had accommodation for twelve children. In reality we only ever housed eight at one time. The children would go to the local schools to which I would drive them and collect them in a large van or bus. They were never to go out alone or unattended. Weekly reports would be submitted by me to the Welfare Officer in charge of the home and I was to try and keep the children out of trouble until they were old enough to make their own way in the world at the age of eighteen.

I would be the housekeeper and house mother, responsible for the happiness and good behaviour of the inmates. In return I would receive a salary, free board and lodgings for my family and John would receive a small payment for helping me keep discipline in the evenings. John would be free to follow his own career as any ordinary father would. The whole atmosphere was geared to that of an extended family rather than an institution. John applied for and was successful in getting a clerical position in the City Council on the administrative side of the African Housing. His hours would be those of an ordinary office worker. He seemed to settle down in this employment.

It all sounded so simple and surely ,with a sensible approach to the everyday problems, I would be able to cope.

We arrived in Ndola when Debra was just four months old. The house had to be furnished and made ready for the first inmates. I quickly realized that it would not be possible for me to drag a small baby out into the heat at all hours of the day and after much thought decided to take Joel's wife Alice, on as a nanny. This relieved me for turning all my attention to the home while keeping an eye from a little distance on my baby. Alice was a boon. Having brought up a considerable family herself she was very capable and Debra was happy being carried on her back in a sling as African babies are. Indeed Debra appeared to thrive on having someone to give her full time attention. If I felt a little jealous at times having to hand over my baby I knew that she was in good hands.

I did in time sneak my own special hour with Debra. She would wake up at three or four every morning and demand tea. We would sit in the kitchen, perched on top of the cabinet, have a talk and a cuddle, and then I would take her back to bed with me. This routine continued for a couple of years and created a special bond between us.

In order to take the appearance of an institution away from the Homestead I used my own table linen, pictures and ornaments in the house. The back veranda, that had been enclosed, I turned into a work come fun room and managed to get a record player and several up to date records. Presentable and comfortable chairs were scattered around. A large table for doing homework took up one corner and, I thought, the whole aspect of the room was pleasing and friendly.

And so we opened our doors to the first two inmates, both girls, Vicky and Dianna. In theory we should have been able to take both girls and boys but while I was there we only had one boy, Michael, for a short while.

I lavished as much attention as I could on Vicky and Dianna. Both were orphans and Vicky had been moved from pillar to post in an extended family none of whom wanted her. After running away several times she came to us at the age of fifteen and I hope that she found some security there.

Dianna was one of twins. Her twin and older sister we didn't meet till much later, when they were ready to leave the country. Dianna had left school and had been working in a photographers when she became pregnant to the African assistant who worked with her. Her baby had been adopted after birth and Dianna was considered to be well over the event according to her reports. She was, however, of fairly low intelligence, not that this distracted from her warm personality. I like to think that Debra helped Dianna to overcome the trauma of having to give up her baby. She was a very affectionate girl and became one of my favorites.

Both girls were considered to be too street wise to be admitted into the other home that was already established in Ndola for children from broken homes.

Vicky was beautiful. She was tall and very shapely even at that early age with long black hair and a slightly coffee colored complexion obviously from some mixed blood in the past history of her family. When happy or angry her dark eyes could flash fire and I realized that of the two this one would be the more difficult to keep on the straight and narrow. She only had to walk down the street to draw attention and she was well aware of the effect she could have on the opposite sex.

Vicky was to attend school for the next six months but I would have to find employment for Dianna which I eventually did. I found this task very difficult as I had to vet the prospective employer and they had to be informed of at least some of the history of the girl concerned.

The home slowly filled up. Some girls came only for a few weeks and then moved on. One such case was Peggy who was not quite sixteen but was three months pregnant. She was keen to marry her boy friend and indeed her mother and the Social Services were in agreement, dare I say as a way to remove the responsibility. I'm afraid I was not, but was overruled and as soon as Peggy turned sixteen she went off to a marriage that lasted two years.

I came to realize that to have a happy home was not enough to keep these girls content and so we devised a system of rewards for good behavior. Visits to the cinema or picnics became the most popular outings.

Michael, the only boy we ever housed, was just ten years old. He came from a broken home and had spent most of his time running away or planning to. He had been in several foster homes where he had remained for an average of three days. He did, however appear to have settled down with us and the reports from his school were satisfactory in that he seemed to be putting in an effort to catch up on his studies. John spent at least an hour with Michael every evening after supper either helping with his homework or playing some game, outside if the weather was good. One evening they were both settled down to a game of drafts. A friendly rivalry had grown up between the two in this game and indeed on this particular night Michael was winning.

"I've got to go to the toilet" he told John. "Don't cheat while I'm gone".

John waited and was busy planning his next move when it dawned on him that Michael was taking a very long time in the toilet.

"Roni" he said "you had better go and see if Michael is alright. Maybe he is sick or in trouble".

A search of the house and grounds proved that Michael was once again on the run. He was found the next day in Lusaka but was not returned to the Homestead. He left us with a feeling of having failed him in some way. We wanted to know the reason why he ran away. All had seemed to be going so well.

As soon as Vicky turned sixteen she left school and I managed to get her a job as a learner hairdresser. She seemed to be very happy there but of course she had to be transported to and from her place of work. This added an extra run in the truck for me and so occasionally John picked her up on his way home from work. As usual I called on Vicky's employer once a month to be sure that all was going well. One month the lady in charge took me aside and suggested that I keep a stricter eye on Vicky.

"I don't want to interfere", she said in a stage whisper "But there is an elderly man who comes to fetch Vicky some evenings and I wondered. "

I had to explain that "the elderly man" was my husband. John was not flattered by this description.

As the home filled up the usual requests from the Department came through to cut costs. This was difficult to do without reducing the standards. One idea I hit on was to do our own dry cleaning. The dry cleaning bill for school clothes was high as I insisted that the girls be turned out in immaculate uniforms. I did not want the girls to look as if they wore second hand clothes. I thought that they had enough to contend with without further stigmas. And so I brought in benzene and the girls and I cleaned the necessary clothes ourselves.

It was at about this time, or a little later, that the atmosphere in the home started to change. We then had six girls resident two of whom were Dimples and Jean. Jean was inclined to swings of temperament bordering on instability of mind. May and her younger sister of eight were admitted much against their will.

Suddenly these four girls displayed the wild ranges of temperament that in the past I had only associated with Jean. Arguments turning to fights when the girls scratched and tore at each other became common in the evenings. The girls refused to do any chore around the house and more often than not those at school neglected their homework. I found myself at a complete loss to understand what was happening.

The fact that John had rejoined the St. Vincent de Paul Society and also the Knights of de Gamma, another Catholic organization, and was now away from home most evenings added to my troubles. I needed the moral support that he was supposed to give me in the evenings when the inmates were at their most tiresome.

May and Dimples ran away. We were not allowed to restrain the children in any way or to physically touch them. John was not at home and all I could do as they walked out the door was to inform the police.

They returned later that night under police escort having been found wandering aimlessly around the town. They offered no explanation as to why they had run away nor did they offer any apology for the trouble they had caused. After the alarm had been set off, the Welfare Officer had spent several hours in the home that night. The safety of the girls had been my main concern as the security situation in the country was not easy and a young white girl alone was prey to all sorts of horrible incidents.

The weekly staff meetings with the Welfare Officers became a nightmare to me. It seemed that all I had to report were misdemeanors and bad behavior. I received very little constructive help from my superiors who took the view that it was all to be expected. I could not agree. It was when I was at my wits end that Dianne came to my room late one night.

"Mrs. Walker," She whispered. "The girls have been sniffing the benzene and that is what is making them do silly things. Please don't let anyone know that I've told you".

"I don't understand Dianna." I said "Why would they do something like that? Surely it must smell awful".

Dianna had to explain to me how they poured the liquid onto a cloth and then holding it to their faces inhaled the fumes. She added that their eyes appeared to glaze over and they did not know what they were doing. She herself had not tried it as she did not like the smell.

Well!! I knew nothing about the taking of drugs or the sniffing of obnoxious fumes and their effects. There was literature that I could study. I learnt the hard way! Reports on the situation were sent to Head Office and for a couple of days the Homestead was overrun by Welfare Workers.

Naturally all benzene was banned from the house, but not to be outdone Jean overcame the lack of this substance by pushing a hose pipe down the petrol tank on the bus and inhaling the fumes from there. No amount of telling these girls how they could kill themselves bought any remorse. Keys were fitted to the petrol tank and John and I spent hours making sure that there was no other substance that could be used as a drug.

One night May walked out of the front door. She was well aware that we could not stop her. We duly followed the same routine. We phoned the police and then the Welfare Officer and then as it was now getting on to midnight we locked all the doors and windows and waited in the darkened sitting room. The remaining girls had been warned not to let May in if she returned. At about 2a.m. she did return and we heard her knock on the window for someone to open it and let her in. Failing to get a response she fell asleep in the summerhouse in the garden. She was very drunk. We obviously could not leave her there but were unable to wake her by calling to her. We were not allowed to physically touch her. And so, I must admit that with a certain delight, we poured a bucket of water over her. May came round with a great deal of spluttering and groaning which I watched without much compassion. We were then able to get her inside and into her bed. There was for me a feeling of satisfaction with our action. Within a couple of days May and her sister were removed from the Homestead.

But the rot had already crept in. Whether out of boredom or just plain cussedness, Jean bought some caustic soda and with Dimples, dissolved some in water and drank it. Alerted by the screams from the back bedroom I ran to find both girls writhing on the floor. Both had been sick which aggravated their pain and injuries. Their burns were horrific. Their mouths and lips were swollen to twice the normal size and everywhere that the corrosive had touched a blister was already forming. I realized that I would not be able to cope with both girls in the van and so phoned for the ambulance.

The wait for it to arrive seemed endless. Both girls were now in shock but besides keeping them warm and talking to them there was nothing else that I could do. I washed off the obvious spills but it was impossible to get any liquid into their mouths. The relief that I felt when the ambulance drove out of our gate was enormous, not because I thought that they were now safe but because there was someone with more experience than me to deal with them.

Eventually after several days in hospital they returned somewhat wiser and greatly subdued. They were very lucky that they did not need to have plastic surgery to their faces or gullets.

When tempers had somewhat subsided I questioned the girls to discover why they had done such a senseless thing. Neither could provide any explanation and I was left with a feeling that it was a spur of the moment decision. And yet they had bought in the caustic soda themselves.

These events rocked my ideas about children just needing love to bring them round and while acknowledging that I had been extremely naive I found myself growing a fairly tough skin. So much so that when Lore who was now going on five and well aware of what was happening in the home, threatened to run away I packed a small case and handing it to her, pushed her through the front door.

"If you want to run away then go" I shouted at her. "I don't want you if you behave like this".

Poor little girl! She went crying down the road but soon came back. She never ever threatened to run away again and remembers the episode to this day. I spent several days in remorse over my action. However I did realize that my nerves were at breaking point and that my judgment in dealing with the problems in the home was becoming warped to say the least. This clearly could not go on.

I more or less begged John to remain at the home in the evenings and resign from his various charity meetings. I pointed out to him that he was receiving payment to stay in at night. As usual my arguments had no effect on my husband.

In desperation, on one occasion, I went to see the priest and told him that John might just a well take his bed down to the church. This had some small success and John's meetings were reduced in number.

Besides the very personal pressures in the Homestead was the feeling of insecurity that prevailed in the country at that time. The bloody civil war still raged across the border now no further than a half day drive from Ndola. Tales of murder, rape, and mutilation trickled in. The ordinary people were starving in their hundreds and thousands were now homeless as they fled from the fighting. Cannibalism was supposed to be rife. After all it was not so long ago that this was the norm amongst some of the tribes. African leaders like Patrice Lumumba disappeared and were never seen again. Ribald jokes about the situation spread through our community possibly to cover the ever present fear that lay in everyone's mind that the war would cross the border.

One story circulated as follows.

"What do you think of Lumumba?" asked one African leader of a U.N. official he was entertaining to dinner.

"Not a bad fellow" replied the officer. "Good" came the reply "Have another slice".

The Swedish Secretary General of the United Nations, Dag Hammarskjol, flew to the Congo to try to bring some semblance of reason to the situation in September 1961. He was to meet various leaders at a small town in the south of Katanga province but his plane lost its' way and crashed in the thick bush only a few miles from Ndola. It took several days for the remains to be found and it was then discovered that some of the passengers of the plane had been alive after the crash although badly injured. An African charcoal burner had stumbled on the wreckage soon after it had occurred but instead of informing the authorities of it whereabouts, he had looted the plane taking anything of value that he could find such as watches and rings from the victims and then disappeared back into the forest. When the plane was finally found one man was still alive but died soon after reaching hospital in Ndola. No one had expected the plane to be so far off course.

Tinned chicken and other foodstuffs, donated by overseas charity organizations appeared in the local African markets clearly labeled "Free gift to the people of the Congo from U.S.A." and sold at knock down prices. This was all evidence of the corruption that was taking place so near us.

Next door to the Homestead was a block of flats. on our side of the separating wall was a line of mango trees. One day Lore burst into my small office.

"There is a nasty boy stealing our mangos" she cried indignantly.

When I went to investigate I found a couple of French speaking youngsters up the trees. Of course I could not speak their language and they could not understand me but I realized that they must be refugees from across the border. We helped them fill a basket with the fruit. When John came home that evening I explained the situation to him and he was able to help the family through the St. Vincent de Paul. Apparently there were only men in the party, a fact that led to much speculation due to the tales we had heard.

The Federal Government began to station troops and extra police in our area, but far from giving us a sense of security this only made us more aware of how vulnerable we were. The growing tide of African Nationalism caused trouble in the African locations and at one time an armed insurrection was expected. All able bodied European men were expected to volunteer their services. One weekend John was sent to guard the local water works on the outskirts of the town. He was given a knobkerry to do the job. This is a very stout stick with a knob on the end, used by the Africans when they went on their hunting trips. The situation appeared to be ludicrous. However, with the build up of the army things calmed down at least on the surface.

After I had been at the Homestead for a year I was entitled to two weeks holiday and it was with great relief that with John and our two girls we went up to Lake Nyasa, as it was then. We flew to Salima, In Nyasaland, now Malawi, in a small plane, landed on a bush airstrip, and were then transported by jeep to Grand Beach on the shore of the lake.

The blue waters of the lake with its' necklace of white sand under the intense blue African sky are as near to heaven as I can imagine. The accommodation was separate chalets built around a central dining hall and administration block. We spent every morning on the beach or swimming in the warm waters. We went goggle fishing and were amazed at the variety and colors of the fish that swam around us. At mid morning tea was bought to us where ever we were by smiling waiters. The food was excellent mostly being fish fresh from the lake. In the afternoon we sailed or walked over the headland to watch the dhows come in from across the lake in Mozambique. From afar they made a beautiful picture with their red sails catching the afternoon sunlight. In the morning they would return across the lake with usually a full complement of passengers. Each passenger paid their fare on the beach and then was carried on the back of the boatman the few yards to the boat where they were handed a bucket. All were expected to bail while on board. Having peered into the interior of the boat with its' few inches of water in which floated all kinds of refuse from decaying fish heads and other indescribable matter, and having received a whiff of the stench there, I came to the conclusion that I would prefer to take the several hundred mile journey by land to reach the other side.

The dhows that plied their trade across these blue waters were the descendants or in some cases the original ones that the Arabs had used when they transported slaves on their way to the coast. It was not so long ago that the slave trade had been halted in Central Africa.

One can imagine the slaves, shackled together, being herded into the dhows and the screams and shouts as they went down into the depths when a freak storm caught the boat in the middle of the lake. These storms are not uncommon and can whip up the usually calm waters into towering waves in a matter of minutes. How many lie at the bottom of these smiling waters?

In the evenings at the hotel, there was usually some entertainment organized from impromptu dances or quizzes, but with so much swimming and sun I was usually in bed at an early hour.

There were no shops in the immediate vicinity of Grand Beach but we did take one trip into Salima. It was really just a local market with the usual police and administrative outpost controlled by Europeans from the British Civil Service.

The market with its' colorful stalls of local vegetables, orange and yellow pumpkins, green mealies, mangoes and pawpaw would have provided an artist with a very tempting subject. But I was no artist. The African women in Malawi wear a graceful kanga or sarong printed in the brightest of colors. The custom is that a woman's legs must be covered. She can quite happily go naked to the waist but to expose the legs is taboo. They wear matching colored turbans on their heads and long ear rings made of brass or copper. Of course the enviable baby is strapped to their backs.

The fortnight's holiday passed much too fast for me and it seemed that in no time we were back at the Homestead with its' problems and trials. But the rest had done us a great deal of good and I faced the second year of my contract with renewed vigor.

I had very little social life while I was at the Homestead. I did get one day off a week when a relief matron took over the transporting of the girls but this usually fell on a weekday and as John had our car I could not leave the premises. We did not have a private sitting room and so it was impossible to get away from the atmosphere of the home.

So when John came home with an invitation to a dinner dance to be held by the Knights of de Gamma, I agreed with excitement. John, as did all the knights, always went to the monthly meetings in full evening dress and so I set out to make a dress that I thought would suit the occasion. I bought some silver grosgrain and sewed a strapless tight fitting dress. I thought it was stunning but in retrospect, as I was so thin, a more bouffant stile would have been better. On the night of the dinner I dressed and the girls hovered around, complimenting me on the dress and offering advice and makeup. I was very excited.

As I entered the hall where the dinner was to be held I stared in horror. All the ladies were dressed in cotton skirts and sandals. My balloon was well and truly pricked and I could not wait for the evening to finish. I just didn't have the aplomb or self confidence to carry off the difference in dress and felt that all the ladies were whispering and sniggering behind my back. My lovely silver dress was consigned to the back of the wardrobe never to be worn again.

The girls, as girls must, attracted boy friends. I realized that I could not keep the opposite sex out of the Homestead and so made a rule that they would be allowed in over the weekend, strictly chaperoned of course, and all to leave at ten o'clock. We arranged parties and barbecues or brais as they are called in Africa.

Vicky fell in love with a young soldier. He obtained permission from his superiors and Vicky from the Welfare Department to get married. My plea to wait a while was ignored and so preparations for the wedding went ahead. They were both so very young. As it was inevitable I swallowed my objections.

I bought the material and sewed Vicky's dress myself. It was of white lace, mid calf length, with a very wide skirt that showed off her small waist to perfection. She wore a short very full veil and to my mind was very beautiful. Lore was flower girl dressed in blue and shared the honor with a cousin of Vicky's. John resplendent in a new suit gave Vicky away. The Homestead was too small for the reception so we hired a hall for the occasion but it fell to me to do the catering. It was a very happy day and Vicky looked radiant.

Dianna's older sister was a police woman who had been stationed in Lusaka. She had never visited Dianna in Ndola. Towards the middle of my second year at the Homestead she made plans to emigrate with the twins to Canada. It seemed a very wise thing to do with the insecurity in Central Africa. But it was with a very heavy heart that I helped get Dianna's passport and clothes together ready for her departure. We both cried a little at the airport but she went off to a new life. For a while we corresponded until I received a request from her sister, via the Welfare Department, that I stop writing. The sister thought that without any ties in Africa Dianna would settle down faster. And so the last I ever heard of Dianne was that she was living in Calgary, but I still treasure a small porcelain horse that she gave me before she left

John and I were now able to purchase a new car. The cars we had owned in the past were always very second hand and the thought of a brand new one was very enticing. After much thought John decided on a Taunus which was the German Ford. It was a beautiful five door estate, green with a white roof. John insisted that I have the honor of collecting it from the garage and driving it home for the first time. It was with great pride that I slipped into the driver's seat and smelt for the first time that unique scent of a new car but I must admit that I breathed a sigh of relief when I arrived home safe and sound without a scratch on the car.

As I came to the end of the second year of my contract I decided that I could not face another. John was happy in his work and we now had some money put aside in the bank. I had lost two stones in weight while at the Homestead and I wanted a more orderly life style in which to bring up my children. Lore was completing her first year at the local Convent and had seen much of the traumas and stress in the Homestead. I did not want her to be in contact with any more. And so I persuaded John that it was time I changed my work. Strangely he agreed and I handed in my notice. However, I was persuaded to take over the old people's home of Insarkwe for six months while the regular matron went on long leave, before I left.

I had no regrets in leaving the Homestead. The two years had been so full of anguish and worry that I thought nothing could ever rival them. My preconceived ideas of young teenager's just needing love had been dashed to pieces and I was disillusioned and perhaps slightly bitter. I considered that I had failed dismally. The Senior Officer pointed out that I had kept the girls from becoming pregnant and that none had committed any serious crime while in my care.

"We could not expect more than that" He said. "The inmates were already on the downward track when we got them and the fact that they had a couple of virtually trouble free years is to your credit"

These remarks did nothing to alleviate the feeling of dejection that I took away with me, and I wondered how society like ours could just write off youngsters like this. What was their future? Well I would have to leave that to wiser people then myself. The lady who took over from me was a qualified Social Worker and so was starting with much more knowledge than I had had when I first started at the Homestead.

Insarkwe was a home run by the Social Services and in theory was to house elderly men and women who had no other means of support than a very meager Government pension. In practice we took several adult waifs and stays that were impossible to accommodate elsewhere.

The home was built in two long lines of separate rooms adjoining a dining room, entertainment room and administration block. All the rooms opened out onto a veranda that ran down the front of the building and were very comfortably furnished with a bed, easy chair, work table and the usual dressing table and wardrobe.

The grounds were pleasant and kept in good order. We had a small cottage to ourselves in the grounds which was too small for my growing family but would do for the six months that we would be there. I had left Joel at the Homestead as Insarkwe already had a well trained staff. He would rejoin us when this short tour was over. Alice continued to come down to me every day as we were not far from the Homestead.

There were several very interesting old characters resident there and I only regret that I did not write some of their stories of 'The Old Days' down. One elderly inmate, Bill, who had remained a bachelor all his life, triggered my imagination. He had worked on the construction of the railway from Livingstone up to the Copper Belt in the early days of the colony. He told of lions taking sleeping men from their tents at night and skirmishes with the Barotse warriors. Unfortunately women were his pet hate and so it fell to John to spend some time with him in the evenings as he was now bedridden. Except for the African staff Bill had no other daily social contact with anyone but John. It was a battle to get his bed made every morning and to dress his leg ulcers. I thought that he secretly enjoyed my ministrations as he never stopped ranting and raving at me while I was in his room. A waiter had to take all his meals into his room on a tray and if he failed to eat it all he would hoard the food in his side table. Once a month he attended the hospital for a check up and on these days the waiter and I would give his room a spring clean, removing all the moldy pieces of bread and worse. When the ambulance once again returned him to Insarkwe and he had been transferred to his bed we would have to put up with his ranting that we had stolen his food "Which he had paid for" until he accumulated another hoard.

All the inmates of Insarkwe had some of their pension deducted for living expenses and were handed the remainder. On pension day most of the able bodied men would disappear into town and returned home drunk once their money was finished. It was a sad existence and I understood their need to blot out the hopelessness of it for a few hours but it was a difficult job to lift them into their beds and the next morning treat their hangovers. We did try to get them interested in card nights or arrange some other entertainment for them but they were very set in their ways and in the six months that I was there I made very little progress.

When I arrived at the home Mabel and Charles were already in residence. Both were in their middle forties but of a very low intelligence. Neither were employable. It seemed at one time that I was always dragging either one out of the other's room at night. This led to very lewd remarks and sniggers from the other inmates much to my blushes. They were obviously both highly sexed and it appeared to me the best way out of this embarrassing situation was to make it legal and let them get married. And so once again I arranged a wedding. This time it was a very small affair with only the inmates of the home as guests.

As I came to the end of this six months we made plans to take an extended holiday in Beira on the Mozambique coast. It was many years since we had seen the sea. We collected Mum on our way through Karoi and then spent a glorious month just lazing on the hot sands of the Indian ocean. I had only seen Mum for a few days while we were on the Copper Belt as there was no room for her at the Homestead and I had not seen Mary and Fred for the whole time. During the last three years Mary Jane had been born and Mary and Fred now had five children. I was impatient to see my new niece. We spent a few days with them on the way down and again on the way back which also made a very welcome break in the very long journey.

On our return to Ndola we rented a house in the avenues and as I was still on leave from the Government I spent a month loving and spoiling my two little girls. I was confident that I would be able to get employment with the Government again when I needed it.

I started to get the most terrible headaches and then started with morning sickness in earnest. Whether the ensuing pregnancy was a result of the change in altitude from the highlands of Zambia to the coastal regions of Mozambique or the fact that we had slept in Mary and Fred's old double bed that they had thrown out after the fifth addition to their family is debatable. But pregnant I was and proved to be very anemic. This resulted in a course of very painful iron injections which did cure the headaches but not the morning sickness that as usual lasted all of my pregnancy.

The political situation in the country continued to give concern and it became obvious that the Federation would be dissolved within the next year or two. John became convinced that his job would be Africanized in the near future. He contacted his old employer in Lusake and after a hurried visit there he came back with glowing accounts of a new contract wherein he would get 50% of the profits from the butcher shop of which he would now be the manager. As usual with John there was no written contract. I knew better than to argue with him or to point out that he had never enjoyed butchering. I knew that if he had made up his mind that was it. And so we moved back to Lusaka.

CHAPTER 9

Lusaka was booming. The army and its wives had arrived en masse and it was impossible to find a reasonable house to rent. All were taken up by the armed forces. We finally ended up with a small two bedroom flat in which it would be impossible to fit another cot for the new arrival. I spent most of my days driving around the town looking for empty houses. I finally found one and rushed down to the agents.

"No", I was told "That house is due for repairs and we don t want to rent it out until the work is completed."

I returned home very dejected, but continued to comb the streets. I knew it was useless to go to any of the other Estate Agents. I had already tried them all. After another month had past, the house was still empty and no work had been started on it. My bump was growing fast and told me that time was getting short. I went back to the agents, looking very pregnant and explained my plight to them

"I can't fit a cot into this flat" I said. "Please, please rent me your house to me if only for a few months"

"Sorry" came the reply. "It is out of the question"

It was then that I burst into tears. It was quite involuntary. I was just at the end of my tether.

"Alright, alright" said the agent. "We will rent the house to you for six months. Please don't cry any more".

The Agent fussed around me. He gave me a cup of tea and there and then prepared the lease for me to sign. I expected him to pat me on the shoulder like a child. I was quite prepared to put up with any patronizing in order to get the house.

I came out of the office feeling ashamed of myself but over the moon in that we now had a house into which we could move straight away. During my marriage I had never been allowed to cry. John considered crying very weak and would get very angry with me if I did. I had always to do my crying behind the closed bathroom door. That afternoon I learnt a very important lesson. Tears can be a very strong weapon for a woman, in a man's world, and not all men view them with the same contempt that my husband did.

I have never again employed my tears to get what I want but it is nice to have this knowledge.

And so we moved into "The Broken House" as Lore named it. Joel and Alice now had reasonable accommodation at the back of the house although as usual there was no electricity laid on to the servant's quarters.

In the September of that year I received a letter from Judy. Our correspondence had been sporadic to say the least but I had managed to see her a few times during the years. She had married a divorced Army Officer called Martin with two sons that he had custody of. Judy had also had two little girls of her own. Martin had left the army and while he was looking around Johannesburg for another career, Judy was to take the children and her father–in–law to Knysna, on the South African coast, for a month. She wondered if I would care to join her. Also with her would be one of her friends who had a small son of four. She would also be taking her cook to help with the work.

In spite of having had a holiday not so long ago, with John's urging, I set out from Lusaka with my two girls and my 'bump' that was growing steadily. We went by train and the journey took four days and nights. We left Lusaka, in the heat of October, dressed in cotton dresses, without any jerseys, when the temperature was rising steadily to the high 90s and arrived in the Cape Province to find snow on the mountains. Keeping two lively children entertained while cooped up in a train compartment all that time was murder. It was such a relief to come to the end of the journey.

The house Judy had rented was built into the side of the estuary and one entered into the top story. It had wooden floors. Judy's father–in–law was housed beneath the main sitting room and could hear every movement that went on above him. With seven children, and three adults the noise was quite considerable and the old man spent most of his days banging on his ceiling with a walking stick.

It rained, and rained, day after day. The washing went moldy, the children became bored and fought continually. They could only go outside if bundled up in waterproof coats and as it was misty they could not be left to go alone. Not only was it wet but it was always cold. There was no heating in the house at all. The cooking was done on a wood fire and the wood was continually wet. Of the five weeks that we were there we had five sunny days. Then the sea sparkled and the world changed.

When the sun did shine we all piled into Judy's estate car and rushed to the beach. There were some wonderful beaches around. One in particular was down a very steep cliff the access to which was about a hundred steps. Except for our party, there was no one else on the beach. We spent an idyllic day there. The children ran on the soft, white sand and Judy and I swam to our hearts content, surfing in the warm waves. Betty, Judy's friend was reputed to have a weak heart and did not swim or lift or do anything much at all, but she was available to sit in a chair and keep her eyes on the little ones.

Going down to the beach had presented no problem but climbing back was another matter. We had all the usual paraphernalia of a picnic to carry and the children were all tired out.

Debby decided that she couldn't climb another step and sat down and cried. I could not move her and so had to carry her up with some of the picnic baskets. She was after all only 2½ years old. That night I could not move because of the pain in my abdomen. Judy and I both thought that I was on the verge of a miscarriage and summoned a Doctor. However, my 'bump' stayed where he was and the pain gradually subsided. The diagnosis was a strained uterus.

I'm sure that we were all very pleased when the five weeks came to an end and we thankfully bade each other "Goodbye". The cook went to hospital with a hernia when he got home. Judy had a threatened miscarriage and when the train finally puffed its' way into the station at Lusake I handed my girls over to Alice and dragged myself to bed where I sank into a deep sleep. I could not wake up, and was only vaguely conscious when I was taken into hospital where I stayed for the next week. The long journey home in the slow train with my two little girls had proved to be the last straw on my over–burdened body. I was diagnosed as having extreme exhaustion. But I recovered.

Mum as usual came up to Lusaka, well in time, for the birth of our third baby but the expected day of arrival came and went with no sign of it. Eventually, when he was two weeks overdue, I was advised to go into hospital for an induction. As usual John was much too busy to take me and with my suitcase I took a taxi. I had begun to realize that my husband was frightened of birth or indeed of anything to do with hospitals and it would do no good to argue about his duty to me as his wife.

It was a week and a long hard labor before my long skinny son weighed in at 9 pounds. He was not well after the birth and as soon as I had given him a quick hug and kiss he was whisked off to the incubator and there he remained for the next three days. Because he had had such a difficult birth I had baptized him in that brief time that I had held him. He was to be called Gavin, (my choice) Thaddeaus (John's choice) after Saint Jude Thaddeaus.

Gavin was born on 17th. February 1963, exactly three years separating him from Debra. I was later to boast that it was due to good family planning but this, of course, was not true.

When we finally arrived home with the new baby, Alice was there expecting to take charge straight away but I managed to stall her until it became necessary for me to find work once again when Gavin was about four months old. This time I found a mornings only job in the Medical Diagnostic Centre, a private firm that was run by Dr. Keith a radiologist.

Besides the X–Ray department we also had a Pathological section for the examining of blood, urine and other bodily functions. I was in my element again and loved the work.

Besides helping to get the specimens I acted as receptionist and did the monthly invoices and ordering of supplies. Although not trained I also helped on occasions in the X – Ray room.

In order to help see in the dark when a screening was taking place both the Doctor and his assistant had to wear dark glasses for a while before going into the examination room. On the first occasion that I was called upon to help with the screening I went in with my heart in my mouth and having worn the glasses, with my eyes ready.

The Doctor called for a photoplate of a certain size and I handed him the wrong one.

"No", he said patiently " I want a 12 x 8."

I fumbled around and came back with another plate. "No", he repeated "A 12 x 8" His tone of voice rising. "But I can't see" I wailed.

"Take off your dark glasses, you idiot." he ordered.

In my haste to get everything correct for the examination I had quite forgotten to remove my dark glasses when entering the dark room.

The Estate Agents who had rented us the house now said that they would have to have it back. This time we were very lucky as a customer of John's agreed to rent us her house. So once again we moved. We had known that our stay in the 'broken house' was only temporary and we were grateful for the time that we had had there. The alternative one would suit us very well.

It belonged to a Mrs. Morrison and so it became the 'Morrison House'. It had a large garden for the children and was in a good location.

In Rhodesia, the Government began preparations for a long war to defend it's borders both from the black north and the British Government who were intent on fostering a black Government on the population.

Police reserves were called up to swell the numbers of that force. Amongst these was Fred, Mary's husband. He was at one time put on road block duty just south of Karoi. Several black political insurgents had attempted to infiltrate over the border and cars were being searched in an effort to put an end to this practice.

One truck, traveling south tried to avoid the road block and ran into the police truck. Fred had been standing in front of the police vehicle and he was sandwiched between the two. He was terribly hurt. A ruptured kidney and spleen, together with several broken ribs and a smashed jaw were amongst his injuries. He was taken into Sinoia hospital and then into Salisbury where he remained on the danger list for several days. Mum looked after the children on the farm and Mary made her home in Salisbury during this time.

John and I took a few days off work and went to help where we could. But there was little that we could do except to give moral support. Fred did eventually recover but walked with a limp for the rest of his life. He would never be a well man again and would never take part in the defense of Rhodesia but we were all very thankful that he was still with us

One morning as I was preparing to go to work, Gavin now crawling and trying to pull himself up, was beside me at the dressing table when he slipped and hit his chin on a tin trunk that stood beside it. I picked him up and held him against my shoulder to comfort him. When I held him away we were both covered in blood. His new front teeth had almost severed the tip of his tongue. Frantic calls to the Doctor ensued. Fortunately, that day I had the car, and with Alice holding Gavin we drove to the hospital as arranged. Of course as Gavin had already had his breakfast we had to wait a couple of hours, before he could be given an anesthetic, in order to stitch his tongue. After I had taken him into the theatre and seen him put to sleep I was told to go home and to return in about three or four hours time.

Alice had been sitting in the car all this time but when I told her that we were going home and would return in a few hours she was very angry that I should even consider leaving Gavin alone there. Like the average African woman she had an inbred mistrust of hospitals.

She got out of the car and sat under the trees. She would not come with me while Gavin was in the hospital and she remained under the same tree until, recovered from the anesthetic, I brought him out once again.

Then Alice opened her arms to hold him and hug him to her rather ample bosom. A big smile broke over her shiny black face and at peace once more we returned home.

Gavin did of course recover although the accident left him with a speech impediment that retarded his talking and would stay with him until much later when he received speech lessons at the age of ten. I always thought his lisp very sweet but then I was his mother after all.

Lore in the meantime was at school at the Convent and Debra would start the following year. They were all growing up so fast.

1963, 1964 and 1965 were to prove very momentous years in all our lives.

The British Government bowing to Black pressure broke up the Federation. Nyasaland gained it's independence and became Malawi. Northern Rhodesia would receive its independence the following year and become Zambia. Serious unrest followed the break up. All British personnel were advised to register at the British High Commission in case evacuation became inevitable.

This left me with a personal dilemma. John of course, having been born in Britain held a British passport but I, as my father had been born in South

Africa held a Rhodesian, and later a Federal one. Now the Federation no longer existed and the time had come for me to get a new passport. In my heart I remained staunchly Rhodesian and watched with horror the various moves of the British to get my countrymen to bow to Black rule. But I had to be practical.

John refused to move south. He was optimistic and thought that there should be good opportunities under the Black Government. Our three children were considered British and if the worst came to the worst would be airlifted out to England leaving me behind. The Zambian Government would in all likelihood put every obstacle in the way of an alien Rhodesian. And so against every instinct, I applied for and was granted British citizenship. I felt like a traitor. John to his credit, left the decision to me and it was to prove the right one in the years to come.

Mum came up to Lusaka on one of her periodic visits. She did not look well and complained of pain in her stomach. Dr. Keith kindly did a barium examination on her but could find nothing very wrong. When she returned to Karoi she was looking slightly better and I concluded that she must just have been run down after all the trauma of Fred's illness.

Christmas 1964 was spent quietly at home in Lusaka. John and Lore had both been ill with flu. On Boxing Day Mary phoned early in the morning to say that Mum was ill and they had taken her into Salisbury to hospital. Mary and Fred had returned to the farm but they thought that I had better come down. I left in the car straight away, taking the children with me, dropped them off at the farm and continued into Salisbury. Mum was in ward six, a ward I remembered well from training days. She looked very ill indeed and had lost the will to live.

"I don' t want to go on any more Roni" she said. "I want to be with Dad".

She had been very lonely on the farm and she was after all a very elderly lady. Life had not dealt kindly with her and she was worn out with hard work. The diagnosis was leukemia and the Doctor, when I managed to see him did not hold out any hope of recovery but thought that it would take a few weeks before the end came.

I slept at night with some old family friends and spent my days at the hospital. I had always planned that I would nurse my mother in her last days but this was not to be and my heart ached because of it. At night I poured out my heart with my tears to the friend I was staying with.

In the meantime I had to be practical. The car needed a new license with the New Year which was only two days away. I would not be allowed to return across the border, with the car without it after the end of the year.

And so I kissed my mother goodbye, picked up the children and returned to Lusaka intending to motor back in a few days. My last words to her were "I've got to go but I'll be back as soon as I can." She just smiled and kissed me.

New Years day of 1965 was filled with telephone calls as I arranged leave from my work and a friend to help John with the children. I wrote a hurried letter to Ann but this remained unfinished as Mary phoned on the morning of 2nd to say that Mum was sinking fast. There would be no time to motor down so John took me to the airport and I flew into Salisbury.

At the hospital found Mum unconscious and unable to recognize me. I stayed by her bed all that day saying the rosary and praying for her. I could not bring myself to give up hope that she would recover even though I knew in my heart that she had willed herself to die.

In the late afternoon Mary, Fred and some of their children arrived. As the evening wore on the ward sister advised us to leave the hospital as she did not think that Mum would die that night. And so we took a room in Meikles hotel. We had not even undressed when the phone rang summoning us back to the hospital. Even though we left straight away the priest was there when we arrived and was reciting the prayer for the dead.

"May the angels lead thee into paradise. May the choir of angels receive thee, and mayest thou have eternal rest with Lazarus"

My prop and my strength had gone. I think that a piece of my heart broke off then. I had loved my mother and had thought that there was no one in the world like her.

My heart went out to Ann, so far away, who had not even known of Mum's illness before she received the telegram saying that she was dead. I retrieved Mum's prayer book from under her pillow and later sent it to Ann.

We buried Mum within three days next to Dad, as she had arranged and John flew down for the funeral. Both Mary and I were amazed at the number of people who came up to us and said that Mum had helped them at various times. She had been greatly loved.

One obituary in the local paper said "The passing of a Great Lady", and she was all of that.

John and I flew home to our children that night after the funeral but I returned to the farm within a few days to help Mary pack up Mum's cottage. She had left no will and indeed except for a few possessions had not left anything of any monetary worth. So we disposed of the belongings as we thought fit and it was only later that we got a wrap over the fingers as it should have all been left until the Master of the High Court had arranged matters. It had been a heart breaking task and one I thought better to be done as soon as possible as the weeks would not soften the heartache.

Of my three children only Lore was old enough to understand what had happened. It was very difficult to tell her that Granny was dead. She had been very fond of her Grandmother and missed her badly in the days following. We cried and mourned together.

CHAPTER 10

The Federation was dissolved in 1964 and Northern Rhodesia was to get it's independence in 1965 and become Zambia under a black Government. There were several unprecedented acts of terrorism committed in the transition period on both the black and white population by the rival black political parties vying for power.

Families of rival political factions were set upon and beaten up. Sometimes their houses were set on fire and the ordinary black population were forced to attend rallies, at gun point, by groups of thugs.

A European mother returning from town, by car, with her three young children were set upon by a screaming black mob and the car was set alight with the occupants still inside it. The children were rescued but the mother later died in hospital. This incident was the first of several that occurred.

The European community began to leave the country, first as a steady trickle and then as a flood, not in a blind panic as in the Congo, but a more or less a planned withdrawal. As the British, who had been recruited in Britain, came to the end of their contract, they received a golden handshake and a free trip back to the United Kingdom. They had been employed to run the Civil Service and the police.

Their positions were filled by Africans often with little or no experience. The mines had employed many South Africans and most of these families returned south of the Limpopo to the Republic of South Africa, their going leaving many gaps in the vital mining industry of the country. The railways suffered the same fate.

As the inexperienced and often drunk, black engine drivers took over the trains there was a spate of fatal train accidents. The situation became so bad that if one wanted to pass a derogatory remark, they would say

"O, go and take a train!".

To those Europeans who had made their homes permanently in the country it was a time of much soul searching. It was impossible to sell farms and the banks, unsure of the political situation, would not grant mortgages for the purchase of houses.

John had firmly made up his mind to remain in Zambia and gamble on conditions returning to normal or better still opening up opportunities for those who were brave enough to take them. What these opportunities would be or where they would come from was anyone's guess. I was not so brave and wanted to return to Rhodesia with the children, John would not consider it. This led to innumerable arguments but as usual I bowed to the inevitable. I then started to press for our own home. House prices had sunk to rock bottom and houses were going for a song.

John and I had come to an unspoken agreement that if we were to remain in Zambia, as he wanted, then we must have a permanent home. Building prices sky rocketed and in any case it was not possible to get a bank loan so the dream of building on the twenty acres that we now held the Title deeds for had to be shelved once again.

I would not settle for just any property, as I was sure that somewhere my dream house on a few acres existed.

We started to house hunt in earnest and after several disappointments found it. The brick built, three bedroom house, stood on ten acres of land, eight miles south of Lusaka on Mimossa Road in an area called Chilanga.

There were several similar plots of land in the vicinity all of the same size and all with houses on them. So we would not be completely isolated but would have neighbors within five minutes walk.

Several fruit trees were already on the land but otherwise it was virtually undeveloped. However it did have two boreholes, one with an electric pump and the other with a windmill. These poured water into a huge reservoir that had been built above ground and would be safe from the children falling in. The property stood on a rise and caught any wind that was blowing thus turning the windmill and providing free water.

The selling price was very reasonable as the owner was anxious to return to South Africa. The transaction would be by Deed of Sale, by which we would pay in monthly installments into the Seller's bank until such times as the country settled down and loans from the banks once more became available.

However, we would have to put down a substantial deposit, which we did not have. The promised bonus from the butcher shop had never materialized and as there was no written agreement it was no use thinking of suing. I had become used to John's business transactions. He apparently thought that to insist on written agreements or to demand to see the accounting books was beneath him.

I took a speedy trip to Karoi and borrowed the money for the down payment from Mary and Fred with the promise that I would pay it back monthly.

This was my debt and I insisted that the property be in my name.

To begin with we would have a very difficult time to meet our commitments, but what was new! We had been there before!

I was overjoyed, and as soon as the move was completed we started to develop our small piece of Africa.

Joel and Alice now had a three room 'cottage' a little way from the main house. As it did not have laid on water, this was one of the first improvements that we made. Alice's grandson, Kalioppo, came to live with them. He was about the same age as Gavin and provided an excellent playmate for him. I did hope that Gavin would pick up the local vernacular from Kalioppo.

We also employed two gardeners. One was Mwanza, a relation of Joel's, and Pieman. Pieman was a very tall African with no education whatsoever, but a willing worker with a very attractive smile that he used to cover his innumerable mistakes. He had a permanent limp either from some childhood injury or disease. This did not hamper his progress at all as his pace was either dead slow or stop.

Mavis Perfect, one of the neighbors came to see us as soon as we arrived. She and her husband George lived a little way down the road and they had four children. George was a very big man who was always shouting at something. He terrified our children but it was just his manner really. Many years later I visited Mavis in Durban. She was then a widow George having died of a heart attack. Mavis said

"He died as he lived – shouting because there was a traffic jam!"

But at Chilanga he was great fun and enlivened any party.

Behind us was an elderly couple, Mr. and Mrs. Evans, who had been there many years. Their sons had grown up and left the country and Mrs. Evans would have dearly loved to have finished her life back in England from where she had originally come. She missed the English way of life and tried wherever possible to bring it to Zambia. She always referred to the evening meal as "Tea" whereas we always called it supper or dinner.

On one occasion she called on me to see the room she had just decorated. Wall paper was not used in Zambia, indeed it was not obtainable there, and our walls were painted with an emulsion paint.

Mrs. Evans had been given a book of wallpaper samples, that must have been very old. She had painstakingly separated the book and glued all the samples to the wall. It looked terrible but I was forced to congratulate her and I felt very guilty afterwards.

As I worked mornings only and had to take both Lore and Debby into school each morning, this proved to be no problem as school finished at 1 p.m. the same time as I did. I did in time take a whole car load of neighboring children, in and out of town, mostly from the Chilanga Cement works which was just a further couple of miles from us.

John still had to get to work very early in the morning and so we bought a small motor bike. He traveled to and from work on this unless the children were on holiday in which case we swapped transport and I took the bike. I enjoyed those rides. They took me back to the days when I rode Chummy's bike.

We did not have a tractor and plough as the ten acres hardly called for this sort of equipment but we did find and bought an old and very heavy rotivator. This 'monster' ran on petrol and cut down the man hours in cultivating the land. It was a Godsend even if I once chewed up John's newly laid water pipe with it. Surprisingly he was very understanding and in future laid his pipes deeper underground in case his wife made the same mistake again.

John, unsure of the gardeners, instructed that they were not to use the rotivator and so most of the digging was left to me. Once started, I found the machine difficult to control and many a night I suffered from aching arms, but I was very proud of the progress that we made.

John laid a new road into the house with a proper camber on it so that there were now no more puddles to drive through in the rains. Then he concentrated on the front of the property, where he built a huge terrace. John spent hours making sure that the surface was even and smooth. Then he covered it with grass. The final lawn was beautiful, velvety and green. His pride and joy. He was often to be found on his hands and knees searching for the odd weeds. But John was never satisfied with it's condition and always strove to improve it.

One day, just before we left for work, he instructed Pieman to take the garden fork and aerate the grass by putting the spokes into the soil and gently lift it up a very little before removing the fork. When we returned that evening to our horror as we drove up the new drive there was no lawn left. Pieman, sure that he had carried out a good day's work, stood leaning on the garden fork a huge smile splitting his black face. He had turned the whole lawn over.

John erupted from the car, with me in hot pursuit intent on saving my gardener from certain death.

"What t t the Hell did you think you were doing?", John sputtered at Pieman as soon as he had recovered his voice.

"I told you to lift the soil just a little bit" "O, solly" said Pieman

"Ini make mistake, solly!"

I had a very difficult task on restraining my husband from throttling the gardener whose smile remained firmly in place.

We never did manage to restore the lawn to it's former glory.

While John was concentrating on the front of the property I developed what I was sure would be a money making project.

When we moved on to the land there were a few banana trees at the back, under nourished and badly neglected. On closer inspection they proved to be of a very good commercial variety, called Cavendish, and I read all the literature that I could find on the cultivation of bananas. I then spent the next six months in increasing the plantation, cultivating, watering and fertilizing the existing trees and transplanting young shoots to fresh ground. I dug new irrigation channels and carefully monitored the water flow between each clump. In no time we were selling to a local factory.

Bananas were usually planted with the bearing tree, the one that was next to bear and a small sucker on one mound. All other suckers are removed. The mature tree only bears one lot of fruit and then dies and so must be removed as soon as the fruit is cut. The bananas are borne on a large ' branch' , the ones nearest the end being the first to mature. The whole 'branch' is cut and taken green into a factory which ripens them chemically so that all the fruit is at the same stage of maturity. Left to ripen by itself the bananas all will be at different stages of ripeness.

I experimented and grew my bananas, several on a large round mound and was able to get more trees into a small space. The irrigation ditch was situated outside the 'mound' and flooded the whole area.

Working with Pieman, who had been relegated to my side of the enterprise, after the terrace fiasco, I transplanted and increased our trees to over a hundred.

The variety of birds that came to nest in the banana trees, never ceased to delight me. They made their nests in the junction where the broad leaves of the tree met the trunk and in the season most of the trees held at least one nest.

Because I grew the trees on a round island, always leaving only three trees to a clump there was plenty of space left without growth. I then planted watermelons there. But although I carefully fertilized them and sprayed them they came to nothing. The following year when Pieman asked what he should do with the remaining watermelon seeds I threw my arm over an area that had had potatoes in it the previous season and was now fallow.

"Throw them over there. " I said, thinking that they would come to nothing anyway.

Uncultivated, and unfertilized, the vines grew at an amazing rate and we had watermelons, to sell, give to our friends, and gorge ourselves on.

The orchard, after pruning, fertilizing and watering, produced good fruit which I also sold. When we arrived there we found that the citrus fruit had a large amount of pith under the skin. After reading several books or the subject we found out that this was due to the low amount of boran in the soil. We applied the recommended dose of this trace element to the ground and we eradicated the thick pith.

There were oranges, tangerines, grapefruit, mangoes end mulberries, planted haphazardly within easy reach of the irrigation channel. In time we sold the fruit.

Then I went into flowers. I imported gladiolus corms from South Africa and sold the spikes to a ready market. Eventually I even sold chrysanthemums but the debudding of these blooms was a never ending task and hardly paid for the work that was put into them.

I kept chickens for our own use and gradually increased the stock. They were reared on the deep litter system and when the grass was removed from the pens it was composted for the garden. Towards the end of our stay at Chilanga I started to rear turkeys.

One evening John returned from the butcher shop with two small puppies tucked into his coat. They had been given to him by a customer and were a cross between a Border Collie and an Australia Dingo. I think that they were the ugliest dogs that I had ever seen. As they grew they proved to be quite untrainable and spent their day running up and down the boundary chasing the odd African that passed. We were not fenced and I seemed to spend my time at home chasing after the two dogs in an effort to save the local population. As guard dogs they were excellent, but I could not tolerate them terrifying the black children on the road. After several very unpleasant episodes I told John that they would have to be put down. He readily agreed but of course was much too busy to undertake the unpleasant task and so it was left to me to take them into the vet.

We did have a golden spaniel called Foggy, who had mated with a terrier of some sort and produced two pups, Patch and Boots, before she was spayed. We really did not need any more dogs.

When we had arrived at Chilanga, only Lore was a competent swimmer and with the reservoir it became important that they all learn to swim well. We discovered a very nice swimming pool at the village of Kafue some 15 miles away. This complex had a shallow pool for children. We took our picnic lunch with us and spent the day there. By the time we left in the early evening Debby was swimming like a duck. I had never seen a child pick up a sport so quickly. As Gavin was only two he took a little longer.

The children swam all year round in the reservoir as soon as I was sure that they were not in any danger. Coming straight from underground, the water was not treated but was pure. In winter a thick, green scum collected on the surface of the water. It amused me to hear Lore one bright winter's day telling her sister,

"You go in first Debby",

Always ready to do her sister's bidding Debby, obeyed and in so doing pushed the scum to one side. The area now cleared, Lore consented to take the plunge. They could of course have removed the scum with the net that always stood ready but this was too much work in their eyes. During this time the girls always had a greenish tinge on their hair!

Gavin, still being too small and not able to swim spent much of his time at the outlet pipe from the reservoir where a large pool had formed. He used to say that he was going to play with 'his friend'. One day I went to investigate this 'friend' and found him fondling a large toad who appeared to be quite at home in his small hands.

Snakes were to prove a problem in Chilanga. Puff adders seemed to thrive in the area. On one occasion, John narrowly missed stepping on one that was sunning itself on the back step. It was dispatched with alacrity. However as we cleared the tall grass we seemed to get rid of most of the reptiles.

With the coming of the first rains John decided that we should plant potatoes on the uncultivated land that remained in the front of the plot. He managed to get hold of some Scottish seed potatoes and everyone in the household turned out to plant the crop.

We had made a bad mistake in not having the soil tested before we started. It proved to heavily infested with eelworm. Although the plants grew and matured when we reaped the crop the majority of them were bad. However because of the shortage of potatoes in the country even these sold. But we did not plant this crop again.

CHAPTER 11

After many months of political maneuvering, which was watched with trepidation by the Europeans across the northern boundary, the Rhodesian Government issued a Unilateral Declaration of Independence from Britain, on 11th. November 1965. The majority of us, after witnessing the disintegration of the public services, under our new Black Government, were in full sympathy with the Rhodesians.

The British Government applied sanctions to landlocked Rhodesia, and the Rhodesians, girded themselves to resist the ever increasing incursions of terrorists across their borders. Strangely enough Rhodesia still continued to rail much needed maize across the border to help feed the Africans in the north.

I found myself in the middle of another moral dilemma. My loyalties rested with my homeland but my taxes were going to help support a Government who was actively engaged in supporting the terrorists.

As I have already stated John was adamant that we stay in Zambia and apart from leaving him and taking the children with me I had no option but to remain also.

We had decided to travel down to Karoi for the Christmas of 1965.

Crossing the border at Chirundu on the Zambezi river, was now a complicated process and passports had to be shown and examined on both sides. Cars were searched, a long time – consuming process.

On this occasion, with the children lying on blankets in the back of our Taunus Estate car, we reached the border at about 7 p.m. expecting to rush through and arrive in Karoi in time for late meal. The evening was hot and humid and the customs shed felt like a furnace. Perhaps it was the heat, as much as the political situation that made the officer confiscate my passport.

"You are Rhodesian born" He said. "You have no right to a British passport"

I was devastated. No amount of arguing had any effect on the officials. I would have to get an exit permit when I wanted to return over the border. My passport would remain with the immigration officials and in exchange I would be given a receipt. I could understand the upsurge of patriotism in the Rhodesians, I felt it myself, but I failed to see how I, as a young woman with three young children, could possibly affect the situation.

John hovered at my side during the exchange between the official and myself, telling me in an undertone, to watch what I said and to control my temper.

It was then too late to return to Chilanga and there was no way to tell Mary and Fred that we would not be arriving. So we had no option but to reluctantly hand over my passport and continue to Karoi.

When we did finally arrive at the farm, Fred treated the affair as a huge joke, but I failed to see any humor in the situation. Trying to get an Official to sign a document over a public holiday is very nearly impossible but Fred knew a friend who knew a friend and I had my exit permit in time to return to Lusaka. I realized that my trips to the farm were not going to be easy in future and it was several years before I returned again. By then the immigration officials had a better understanding of the situation and were more lenient.

While at the farm we were instructed in the use of firearms and took part in the target practice that had become a weekly occurrence for the isolated farmers and their wives. I had never before handled a gun.

All the farms and mines had huge white numbers painted on an area clearly visible from the air, so that they could be easily identified in case of attack. Two – way radios were installed in all isolated houses to enable the occupants to call for help in case of attack.

Twice daily a news update was broadcasted over the air on this radio and was avidly monitored.

All able bodied men were recruited into local armed groups, called partu, ready for any call to help defend neighboring farms, and mines, in the event of terrorist attacks. Many of these men also served a three month stint in the army once a year, leaving their wives alone to run the farms.

Eventually, as the war stepped up and terrorist attacks on undefended, isolated homesteads became more common, high security fences were built surrounding the homesteads and all windows would be protected by grenade screens. No one would travel after dark for fear of attack by isolated groups of terrorists.

However, the general atmosphere was one of optimism. They were fighting for a way of life and I was proud of them if not a little envious.

When I said 'Goodbye' to my sister, when it was time to return north, it was with a very heavy heart.

CHAPTER 12

We called our home St. Lucia after Mum, whose name was Dolores Lucy.

Being so near to town, it was an easy run in a car for friends from Lusaka to visit on a Sunday, and it was very unusual if we did not have visitors who stayed on for a light meal in the evening. We also became friendly with people in the area. Chilanga Cement was not far away and had a community of its own. We joined a club there and made many friends. Also in the area was Mount Mkulu research station, a Government Institution, which researched the growing of crops. At that time they also employed several Europeans who gave us invaluable advice on the many problems that faced us in our new project.

John was still a member of the St. Vincent de Paul Society but did not spend very much time with them now, due to our distance from town. One Sunday morning after Mass the priest introduced us to Jim and Joan Doyle.

The Doyles had been farming in Kenya on their own fairly large estate when they were forced to leave because of the Mau Mau. They had packed their seven children and all that they could get into a V. W. Combie and journeyed down to South Africa. Jim was an agronomist and Joan a competent bookkeeper.

Disillusioned with South African politics, they had come up to Zambia and were once more endeavoring to get on their feet. They were, at that time, all living in a two roomed house and were finding life very difficult. Their eldest daughter was now a nun and their eldest son had entered a seminary to become a priest. These two had remained in South Africa but the remaining five children all of school age were with Joan and Jim. Jim had no work yet and money was very short.

We took the family back to St. Lucia where the children swam to their heart's content and gorged themselves on the fruit.

Eventually Jim started a business, advising the Government on agriculture problems and Joan found work doing the books for several private firms.

Ted and Pat Lowe were also regular visitors. We had met them when we were last in Lusaka, in fact Ted and I had worked together at the Government Mechanical Workshops.

Ted and John became interested in a farm that was for sale on the banks of the Kafue river. I was not particularly worried as I knew that neither of the men would be able to raise the finance but they enjoyed themselves making plans.

We traveled down one Sunday to view the farm. The house was a stone built, one roomed cottage, about a hundred yards from the banks of the river. The wife of the farmer who was selling was an old woman and she spent a long time regaling me with stories of the hippos ravaging her garden at night. We went for a walk along the banks of the river and watched the hippos playing in the water, I saw a leguaan for the first time as it slid out from almost under my feet and slid with hardly a ripple beneath the waters.

The Kafue has a very big population of crocodiles and the banks of the river provided many areas where they basked in the sun during the day with their mouths agape. No, I was not, and would never be, prepared to live in such close proximity to these reptiles.

There was very little arable land on the farm and what there was, was situated on a plateau some distance from the homestead. There were no farming implements such as tractors and ploughs.

We returned home and I was confident that even John would not consider the purchase of this property. However I had failed to recognize signs of restlessness that were stirring in John. I was very happy with my life as it was and thought that John was too.

One evening as John was returning from work on the bike, he delivered a parcel of meat to a neighbor and was set upon by two dogs. He was knocked off his bike. He had not been traveling very fast so it was not the speed but the angle of his fall that broke his leg. At last someone heard his calls for help and sent for the ambulance. John was lifted into hospital in a two ton truck. When, eventually I was informed of the accident, I hurried into the hospital where I was informed that he had broken the head of his femur.

The following morning, during an operation, a pin and plate was inserted and screwed into the bone. In this way the fracture would heal very quickly but he would be in hospital for a couple of weeks and would be absent from work for six or seven weeks more.

When I told John's employers of his accident, they took the view that as he was not at work at the time, they were not liable to pay for any sick leave. I left the shop angry and very, very bitter.

But being angry would not solve the financial position that we were now in. I realized that my idyllic life style would have to change. I saw an advertisement for a full time job in the Anglo American Chartered Exploration Company and applied. This Company employed men to travel over the country and take samples of rock every few yards. These samples were then plotted on a map, thus giving a survey of possible minerals deposits from all over the territory. The samples were sent into the laboratory where I would work, crushed, fired and the results were recorded on a film that we would monitor on screen. The minerals showed up on this screen as different densities and thickness. The work would become very boring but the pay was extremely good.

On the afternoon that I was to have my interview for the job, I left the house with plenty of time to spare. I planned to go on to the hospital to visit John after the interview. As I traveled in at a reasonable speed a car with two Africans passed me. It crossed my mind that I should go a little faster. I disliked being passed.

I rounded a corner on a notorious 'S' bend and could not believe the carnage that I saw before me. I slammed on brakes got out of the car, and with my heart in my mouth I surveyed the scene. The car that had passed me had hit an oncoming one head on. I ran to the nearest car, which was the one that had passed me on the road. The two Africans appeared to have no injuries but were sitting still in shock. A body from the second car lay sprawled some distance away. It was a young teenage lad, I ran to him, discovered that he was breathing and had a pulse but was unconscious. I turned him over to prevent him from choking and hurried to the other victims. The driver of the car was screaming but I could find no injuries. He appeared to be in his middle twenties. One young lad lay beside the car his head at an unnatural angle to his body. There was no pulse. He was obviously dead. In the back of the car a third young lad lay, bleeding from his nose and ears a sure sign of a broken neck. His dark brown hair contrasted starkly with the pallor of his face. The front seat had been pushed back onto his legs and I could not move him. He was, however breathing and I held him in my arms, supporting his head on my breast while trying to keep his airway open. His breath came in short gasps and his blood soaked into my dress as it slowly drained his life away. I held him in my arms as he died. The tears were streaming down my face and I was stunned by the enormity of the tragedy around me. I tried to pray but all I could say was

'O God, O God".

The driver had got out of the car and was walking around. The only sound was of escaping steam from the smashed–in engine. On the shelf behind me a suitcase had burst open spewing out it's contents, amongst which was a bible, the pages slowly turning in the breeze that came through the shattered window. Far away a dove called.

I gently laid the lad down on the seat and went to the other victims. I wondered why help was not arriving. I thought that I had heard a car pull up and then drive away.

After what seemed a lifetime but in reality was only a little while several cars arrived. I directed the occupants to the boy who was still lying in the tall grass, gave my name and address to the police when they arrived, and then got into my car and drove to my interview.

After a quick wash I apologized for the lateness of my arrival, explaining the circumstances, and left the building with the job secured.

As I entered the ward where John was, the two casualties that were still alive from the accident were being brought in. I sat beside John and after talking for a few minutes I burst into tears. John, thinking that my tears were for him, was all concern. But in reality it was just delayed shock.

Eventually I learnt that the three teenage lads were from boarding school and had hitched a lift home, for the weekend. They had all come from families at Mount Mkulu. The driver of the car had been speeding and taking the corner too fast, had swung out to the wrong side of the road. The Africans in the second car never had a chance. If I had quickened my pace it might so easily have been me in that accident.

The scene would come back to me for many a night and I would lie awake and wonder if I could have done anything to save those young lives.

I had left the accident without any knowledge of the names of the young lads, but the mother of one of them came to see me in the weeks that followed. I could not tell her if it was her son that I had held in my arms. I think that I understood how she must have been grasping at any information to help ease her pain.

I remained at Chartered Exploration for a year. Every morning I took my children and some from Chilanga Cement, into school and one of the mothers brought them home at lunch time. Gavin remained at home in the care of Alice.

Towards the end of the year Chilanga Cement started a bus for the school children but this was to be only for their employees. I was very annoyed and complained bitterly. However, in order to overcome a very awkward situation they offered me a job in their accounts section. The pay would be better than I was getting in town but as I explained I was no accountant. But I was quick to learn. And so once again I started a new career.

John had left the butchery some months previously and had found employment at a factory near Chilanga. And so we were set up once again, or so I thought.

The Zambia Government, alarmed at the rate that the European farmers were leaving, decided to open large tracks of virgin land in the North East of the country in an area called Mkushi. This land would be subdivided into tobacco and maize farms and offered on a tenant basis to men with a proven record of farming. Financial assistance would be given as seasonal loans to produce the crops until such time as the farm was self supporting and there would be grants for capital development. The land would never belong to the tenant. There were already some scattered farms in the area that had been started a few years previously. All the prospective tenant had to provide was a three ton truck as there was no transport in this part of the country.

Jim Doyle drew John's attention to the scheme and together they went to inspect the area. They came back with glowing reports.

To John this was a chance not to be missed. I was horrified that he would once again disrupt our lives in this way. We had worked so hard on this piece of land and it was just beginning to pay it's way. We were very comfortable and the children were happy. No argument that I put forward had any effect on him whatsoever. In tears I pointed out that the children would have to go to boarding school. He replied that all farmer children, including my sister's went to boarding school.

He applied for the scheme and was accepted.

In order to get the truck, he insisted that I put the house up for sale and was ready to accept the first offer that was made. At this, I dug my heels in, and after negotiations and bargaining I secured a selling price of double that which we had paid.

It was a very distressing day for me when I went into the lawyers office to sign away my home.

I never saw our piece of bush until we actually moved out to Mkushi as the children came down with chickenpox, one after the other and I was not able to get away.

The farm that we were going to would be approximately 3000 acres in extent, would have twenty acres cleared and would have a borehole on it. That was all.

CHAPTER 13

As soon as the money from the sale of the house came through and I had repaid the loan to Mary and Fred, John went into town to collect his truck. It was an Izzu diesel and John informed me

"You'll never be able to drive it Roni. It's much too heavy."

I regarded it with a certain amount of distaste. It represented my home after all.

Then having given up his job John drove to the farm and spent several weeks arranging a labor force, contracting for bricks to be made and installing a very large tank on a steel stand for the water. Eventually a large reservoir would be built to serve the farm. Tractors, trailers and farm implements had already been sent out to the farm by a private contractor.

John returned to Lusaka fired with enthusiasm and helped me to pack up or store the furniture from the house. I could not match his optimism and wandered around the garden as if to imprint each detail on my mind. I had loved this our first real home and faced the future with a feeling of impending doom.

Finally the day of our departure arrived. I said goodbye to Joel and Alice.

"Why is the Boss moving again?" Joel had asked. "He has a good home here"

I was unable to answer him.

"We will not come with you to the bush" he said. "There have been too many moves."

I was so sorry that they had decided this way but I did understand their reasoning. This move was the last thing that I wanted after all. I had found employment for them and I was sure they would be happy there but I would miss them dreadfully. They had become a part of my extended family, and together we had shared many happy and sad times. The children, especially Gavin, who regarded Alice as a second mother, would also miss them. Kalioppo would grow up without Gavin and Gavin would lose his first 'best friend'.

However, Pieman would come with us. I had become strangely fond of the "old devil" as I called him. His saving grace was a sense of humor and his ever ready smile.

Lore being the first to recover from the chickenpox was already at Mkushi with the neighbors Des and Helen Straw. They had generously accommodated John for the last few weeks and we would spend our first night in Mkushi with them.

Some of our household goods had already been taken out to Mkushi and the rest were now packed onto the truck together with boxes of provisions. There would be no fresh meat, vegetables or milk until we could provide these commodities from the farm or purchase them whenever we managed to get back into town again.

Our mattresses covered these goods and the African driver's wife and small children were perched on top together with all their bundles and suitcases. Much like the cherry on top of the cake. I closed my eyes to the fact that they were sitting on top of our unprotected bedding. The journey would take four to five hours and no African baby wore a nappy!

The driver whom John had employed quite recently, had been instructed to wait for us at Broken Hill, later to be called Kabwe, a town approximately half way to the farm, so that John could check that all was well with them.

Feeling very much like an Afrikaner Voortrecker, I packed into our covered wagon (our estate car), two children, two cats, who had been sedated by the vet and then tied into hemp sacks, three dogs, blankets, food and other items that I considered vital at that time.

On my lap, in a shoe box, would travel six day old turkey chicks that were all that I was allowed to take from our large poultry stock.

As the car drew away from the house, and started down the long driveway I turned my head and watched as the yellow walls and black roof were slowly obscured by the dust that billowed up behind the wheels of the car. The tears started to spill over onto my cheeks.

"You're not crying" John asked in an incredulous tone of voice.

"No" I lied "It is just the dust".

The four and a half hour journey started late, and on arrival at Kabwe, as Broken Hill was renamed, there was no sign of the truck. After a meal at a cafe there, we continued on our way. Sixty miles further on we arrived at the village of Kapiri Mposhi. This village was just a collection of Indian shops clustered around a railway siding but it did have a very nice pub, run by a European family, that I would become familiar with in the months to come. Here we turned off the tarmac on to the Great North road, that was really just a sandy track with at times the grass meeting over our heads.

It was at this stage that we met up with the corrugations on the road. Due to the amount of traffic and lack of upkeep, the dirt road had deteriorated into a series of ridges. In order to avoid the bone jarring impact of these ridges it was necessary to keep up a considerable speed so that the vehicle literally skimmed across the top of them. There was a thick cloud of dust in our wake and it was impossible to overtake any vehicle in front as there was no manner in which you could see through the dust that was billowing up behind it.

After about twenty miles of 'The Great North Road', we turned off onto an even rougher track that led eventually, to the block where the farm was situated. Thirty miles from our destination and just as the swift dusk was falling disaster struck. The back window of the car gave up with a thud and sank into the door. The dust came in in a thick yellowish cloud coating everyone and everything, and making breathing very difficult.

Although we tried to raise the window it refused to budge.

John, already uneasy because we had not met up with the truck, began to rail at fate. The cats woke up and their pitiful cries filled the car. The children, tired out with the long journey, began to cry which started the dogs barking and I fell into a fit of hysterical laughter. In this manner we eventually reached our destination, covered in the thick yellow dust only our eyes showing any color. What a sight we must have looked!

As we opened the car doors the dogs made a dash for freedom and meeting the resident dogs were soon fighting. Greetings were delayed as we all endeavored to separate the animals. As we let the cats out of their sacks they made a bee line for the bush around the house and it took several days to find them again.

In spite of our catastrophic arrival we were greeted very warmly by Des and Helen whom I had not met before. A hot bath and food soon restored our good humor but my feelings of gloom persisted. However it was lovely to have Lore with her happy smile to welcome us.

In the bright sunny morning we went to Pandora's Box, as the farm was named. As I looked at the grass hut that John had prepared for us I sent up a silent prayer to Mum to help me through this ordeal. I had a distinct sense of history repeating itself. I felt like bursting into tears but John would never have tolerated that and would have only added ridicule to my feelings of dejection. I realized that there was nothing to be gained from these emotions and decided that I had better pull myself together and make the most of our 'new world'. In time I became very fond of this little bit of Africa.

The truck with its precious load had arrived at the farm the previous evening safe and sound and the driver was dispatched back to Lusaka for further vital building supplies and fertilizer. The truck would make a twice weekly journey, but I would, in time, replace the African driver as we discovered that we could not depend on him to return on schedule. After taking careful records of the mileage, we found that he had been using the truck to conduct his own private transport business. He was fired. There was now no one to drive the vehicle and bring out the vital building supplies.

"I can't leave the farm Roni, so you will have to do it". John announced.

So much for the truck "being too heavy for me!" His new toy had lost a little of it's glitter, by now!

The hut was just a large room made by poles erected within a foot of each other and the intervening spaces were filled in with grass. All cooking would be done on an open wood fire. Water would have to be carried several hundred yards from the bore hole. The paraffin fridge resided outside under its own grass shelter, in case its flame should set the shack alight. Lighting would, of course be provided by paraffin hurricane lamps.

Most of our furniture remained in Lusaka until such time as we had adequate accommodation for it and we would 'make do' with camp chairs.

The loo was a classic! About fifty yards from the hut John had had a deep pit dug into an ant hill. This was surrounded by a grass wall without a door, open to the heavens. Latrines had to be over six feet deep to prevent the flies from breeding. We discovered this fact, to our horror, after two of the children received nasty bites on their bottoms from the blue bottles. Usually the top of the pit was covered by a seat built over the hole and afforded a modicum of comfort but not this one! Unfortunately due to the lack of smooth timber ours was covered by branches newly cut from the trees. I concluded that one was supposed to squat on the rough bark, some of it decidedly prickly. Anything more inducing to constipation is hard to imagine. There was no manner in which one could exclude the various "wild life" in the form of spiders, centipedes, lizards, or the occasional snake from wandering in. This "long drop" was the first thing on my list for renovation.

For as long as I could remember paraffin was delivered in two four gallon tins incased in a wooden box. These boxes proved invaluable. They ended their days as furniture amongst other things. Two lines of boxes placed on top of one another and then joined by a rail across the top made a passable wardrobe, with cupboards on either side, while others became tables or chairs. The first available empty box went to providing a reasonable seat for our loo.

The season was on us and although the rains were not expected for a couple of months the seedbeds for the tobacco had already been started and needed constant attention. The lands had to be ploughed, ridged and fertilized ready for the young plants when the rains came.

For this first year we would only plant twenty acres of tobacco, and if possible enough maize to feed our labor force. John was too busy on the farm so any improvements in our living conditions were left to me.

"After all," as John pointed out, "You have Pieman to help you".

My list of priorities lengthened. After the 'long drop' would come water delivered to the shack. The water tank had been erected on a high steel stand and I scrounged a very long piece of two inch polythene pipeline which would in time be used for irrigition. This came from the outlet pipe in the tank and was was laid over the top of the ground and ended at a grass enclosure within a couple of yards of the hut.

To the end of this pipe I tied a rope that was then thrown over an overhanging branch of a tree, that grew conveniently close, pulling the end of the pipe with it. This made the end, happily, higher than the tank. In order to get water one merely lowered the rope and cut off the supply by hoisting it over the branch again. In the middle of the day the water coming from this pipe was almost boiling but as the day cooled so the temperature dropped. It provided us with a shower and also with water "on tap", or rather 'on pipe'. Eventually the innovation of hoisting up the end of the pipe was replaced by a stop cock which made life even easier.

We had not been on the farm for more than two days when we received the first visits from other farmers in the area. Some came from as far away as twenty miles and all brought a box of vegetables or fresh milk. The community welcomed us with open arms and I have never since experienced the sense of belonging as these people instilled. We were all 'up against it' and everyone helped where they could. They were the salt of the earth . No one complained when the tea tasted of smoke, due to the open fire nor did they eschew the tin mugs it was offered in. Everyone had been through this stage themselves.

The soil in Mkushi was a very sandy loam and due to the heat the trees were very tall and for the most part thin with a canopy of leaves at the very top. At this time of the year they were bare and there was no shade to be found anywhere. Eventually they would put forth beautiful red to pink leaves that slowly turned to green, but before the rains they gave very little comfort from the intense heat. The grass grew to a height of six or seven feet except in the vleis (somewhat like a meadow) that ran with water in the rains and were covered with a short tough grass when in season puts forth its seeds and took on a pink sheen. In the late afternoon sunshine it caused the vlei to 'glow'.

Between the trees the inevitable ant hills raised their conical mounds, bare of grass, sometimes to the height of ten feet above the ground level, and many had to be leveled when the field was prepared for planting but usually the land was just ploughed around them. However, Mkushi was spared the bamboo that was a scourge further west.

A vegetable garden had a very high priority on my list of improvements and Pieman and I started clearing the scrub and grass from a large area of land with badzas. This garden implement, very like an upturned hoe, was regularly used by the Africans.

Pieman was used to me working in the garden with him but thought it should be below a European woman to work as an African.

"No other Nkosi work like you do" He said.

I took this as a complement but if it was meant as one was debatable.

As this was going to become the permanent garden, it was situated some distance from the hut, in the approximate region of the house that would one day be built. In order to keep out the smaller wild life it had to be fenced. John after having seen my hands torn by the barbed wire lent me two men from the tobacco gang to help with the fencing.

There was no way, however that we would be able to exclude a troop of baboons that lived in the vicinity, nor the two legged vandals that resided in the farm compound.

I started the vegetable seed beds, near the hut, with seeds that I had brought out in the car with me. The soil, in Zambia is so fertile and the hot climate so conducive to growth, that in no time the seedlings were ready to plant out and I proudly produced our first salad one night when I had only been on the farm for two months. Admittedly the crop could have been left longer to mature, but it tasted very sweet to me after having to eat the limp vegetables that were bought from town and by the time we ate them were well past their best.

I also planted seeds from fruit trees such as guavas, pawpaw, mango and mulberry. In just eighteen months we were picking fruit. It was my intention to eventually line the farm roads with mango trees as they were very easy to grow and the fruit was much enjoyed by the laborers besides having a very high vitamin content.

The first kiln of bricks had been completed and the building of the first long low barn for curing the tobacco was well under way. However the rains were getting closer and closer, and it was obvious that the hut would not withstand any storm. As so many farm buildings were required we decided that the tractor shed would be constructed next and we would live in that until such time as it became expedient to build ourselves a reasonable house. It might not be luxury but would be heaven compared to the dusty grass shack.

The children, in the meantime were enjoying life to the full and running wild over the bush, exploring their new surrounds, helping the brick makers in their tasks, making mud pies, and generally getting in the way as children do.

September, and the end of the school holidays came. We had arranged that the two girls would finish the school year, which ran from January to December, while staying with Jim and Joan in Lusaka.

Secretly I felt that Jim should take much of the responsibility for the disruption in our lives.

It was with a heavy heart that Gavin and I took the girls back to Lusaka. We had never been separated before and although it was for only three months, and I would see them from time to time during this period, it was a hard break and I shed many a tear as we drove home without them. I realized that this was to be the first of many times that I would have to leave them.

"Never mind, Mummy" said Gavin, his hand stroking my arm. "You still have me"

I wondered for how long.

CHAPTER 14

Pandora, was a three thousand acre farm. It was not very big in comparison to the average farm in Mkushi and it was a long, narrow strip of land covered in thick bush. Across the road which bordered it on the South side lay a very big African Reserve. These reserves had been set up by the previous Government to protect the land for the Africans and contrary to popular belief was just as fertile and arable, in the beginning as that which adjoined it.

The farm had several ridges on it separated by vleis, that in the rain ran with water, but there no rivers.

Several sites could have been chosen for the bore hole, but when the contractors had been in the district they took the first site inside the boundary that they found and had sunk the hole in the extreme western corner of the farm.

Because the water was situated here we would have to start to develop the land and all the farm buildings would have to be erected around this area, instead of being centrally situated. This would in time cause some difficulty and expense as it would add to the time and distance in transporting machinery and labor. But this was how it was and we had to accept the situation.

The African labor force, most of whom had been recruited locally, now totaled some 40 men who, with their wives and children were accommodated in traditional grass huts in a compound. Each family was allocated a plot of land on which to grow their own vegetables, but as was the custom we would be responsible for providing maize meal, beans and kapenta, a small fish coming from lake Nyasa in the north. The fish were dried and transported in sacks and formed a protein rich substitute for meat which was difficult to transport

The custom of providing rations to the labor force was first started, many years previously, to ensure that the wives and children of the laborers were fed, as the men tended to spend any cash they received on beer. This had later become law.

Each morning I held a clinic outside the shack, and dealt out various medicines for the common ailments that beset a rather backward people. The babies with their solemn faces and huge dark eyes were a delight and I took time to coax a smile from them. Many were prone to ringworm which I treated with a purple dye and it was not unusual to see little heads with purple splotches peeping out from the sling in which they were held on their mother's back. Because the family cooked on an open fire, often in the close confines of the hut many of the children suffered from burns as they were continually rolling or falling into the embers of the fires.

I suppose that the most common ailment among the children was gastro enteritis from the very unhygienic conditions in which they lived. I found that the best way to treat this ailment was to deny all food and keep the child on Coca- cola. I did not always feel confident in dealing with the more serious cases that appeared outside our door, but when confronted with a very sick baby that was held in the arms of it's frantic mother it would take a harder heart than mine to turn them away. It was not possible to transport all to the clinic and to send them away knowing that they would have to walk the many miles was unthinkable and so I did the best that I could.

There were no schools in the vicinity and the majority of the people were illiterate unlike those Africans who lived nearer the town centers or mission stations. Perhaps later I would start a very small school for the younger children, I thought.

Once a fortnight, in turn, one woman, from the compound, would brew a forty four gallon drum of African beer from the roppocco (a cereal) the farmer had provided. Then on the Saturday night the drums and singing would continue until the early hours of Sunday morning. The rhythmic beat of the drums that continued on and on interspersed by the shrill squeal of the tin whistles that accompanied them, was carried on the still night air and there was no escaping the invading sound. No pillow was stout enough.

When they finally stopped the silence was deafening until the usual chirp of the crickets and the croak of the frogs in the nearby vlei once more dominated.

In order to have a workforce on the Monday morning, my clinic opened on the Sunday! Besides dealing with sore heads and upset stomachs, there were usually an assortment of knife and bite wounds. I became quite proficient in body stitching.

Although, in hospital, I had watched Doctors performing this task I had never before done it myself and in the beginning I lacked the equipment. I had to start with an ordinary sewing needle and cotton that I sterilized in boiling water. I used my thimble to push the needle through the tough skin. There was no local anesthetic but most of my patients on a Sunday morning were more or less anaesthetized from the amount of alcohol they had consumed the night before. As the weeks wore on I did buy in some surgical needles but I never managed to quite get the cat gut to tie as tight a knot as the strong cotton.

Pieman, my gardener, had brought his wife out from Lusaka when he came to the farm but she had decided that the bush life was not for her and had returned to the city. This left Pieman a very eligible bachelor and he filled his hut with a succession of comely maidens some of whom were already spoken for.

The Saturday night beer drink afforded an opportunity for his roving eye to wander over the women in the compound much to the distress of the other men there. He therefore attended the Sunday clinic as a matter of routine and bore many examples of my handiwork with a needle.

"This sort of behavior has got to stop Pieman" I said to him one Sunday morning while I was tending to his wounds.

"One day some man is going to knife you and I won't be able to help you"

"O no Inkosikus" he said. "My muti is much too strong" and from under his shirt he pulled what resembled a piece of blackened cardboard but turned out to be some skin from a crocodile. With this to protect him Piemen felt safe from any mishap.

It was strange to think that had we still been in Lusaka, Pieman would probably not have trusted in this primitive safeguard, but he appeared to have 'gone back to the bush' since arriving in Mkushi, and I wondered how very thin his veneer of civilization was.

Muti could be purchased from any nganga or witch – doctor and was made from dried herbs or other peculiar ingredients. Woe betide any African who woke in the morning to discover that someone had placed 'muti' outside his door. He would be convinced that he was now bewitched and would disappear with his family. His vacant house would not be occupied by any other laborer and would eventually be burnt to the ground.

One Sunday morning, in the early hours we were woken by a loud thumping on the door. Thinking that there had been some domestic dispute in the compound as there had been a beer drink that night, John went to the door. There stood a very drunk laborer with one hand over his mouth and in the other hand a piece of what resembled raw meat.

"What do you require?" asked John, in his faulty Chinanza (The local vernacular)

"Mmmmm Mmmmm" said the African pointing at me with his bloody hand and then drawing it up to his mouth. On careful inspection and after much difficult explanations it became clear that he and his wife had had an argument and the wife had bitten off his lip. He would now be pleased if

I would sew it back on to his face again!!. Unfortunately this was beyond my meager capabilities

As the nearest Government clinic was some 70 miles away I eventually found myself treating Africans from the reserve, ruled over by a Chief, which bordered our farm. As the patient had usually already been treated by the witch-doctor to no avail, I found these cases increasingly difficult and often sent them away to the clinic.

When land clearing began there were several instances of snake bite. These cases I had to keep under observation, after administering the snake bite serum. This was difficult in the early days as there just was no room and the victim often had to lie under the roof overhang. When the house was built I converted a back store into a temporary hospital ward. I was fortunate in that there was never a death on our farm.

I had never been trained in midwifery and although there were a few births on the farm they were attended to by the local women. However on one occasion an African man arrived on his bicycle. He had traveled many miles with his wife sitting on the crossbar. She had begun labor several hours before and the baby had lodged in the birth canal and would not move. When I examined her I could see the baby's head but according to the man it had been like this for a fair time. I realized that there was nothing I could do and so drove up to the clinic with her. The car journey was bad enough but how she had survived the bicycle trip was beyond imagination.

The building of the tractor shed, where we were going to live progressed slowly. It would have a deep pit in the middle, for the servicing of the vehicles. This would be covered with planks, and the two very large doors at the entrance would be big enough for the tractors to come through.

We anxiously watched the clouds build up each afternoon and told each other that the rains were not due for another month, if we were lucky. But lucky we weren't.

One Sunday evening the heat became increasingly oppressive Sitting outside the shed John and I watched the lightning as it lit up the distant clouds.

John said "I don't like the look of these clouds"

and he drove the car up to within a couple of feet from the door of the shack.

We went to bed and listened to the thunder cracks coming ever nearer. The wind increased and seemed to swirl around the shack. I lay in my bed and optimistically thought that we would be safe and dry. At about 10 o'clock the heavens opened and the hut was awash in less than five minutes. The water just poured in as if there was no roof at all. The blankets had been stored under the mattresses, to keep them relatively dust free. In the pitch dark, I grabbed one and wrapped Gavin in it and with another over my head made a mad dash for the car with Gavin in my arms. John climbed into the beck seat. We were both soaked through but Gavin had remained dry. John and I stripped off our soaking pajamas and then started to shiver in the sudden drop of temperature that follows the rain. We spent the rest of the night passing Gavin between us as he had the only dry blanket.

The morning dawned fresh and beautiful as it can in the tropics. At first light we sneaked back into the shed and rescued a suitcase of dry clothes from under a bed.

However the contents of the hut were just one sodden mass and as the heat of the day increased everything began to smell. The day was spent in drying out what we had managed to salvage in order to prevent a thick green mold from developing.

The majority of the African huts had proved to be waterproof and the men from those that were not spent the day repairing the damage watched over by the very critical eyes of their wives.

The completion of the tractor shed was now vital and the African builder was still working on the roof when we moved in with only bare brick walls and windows with no glass. But it was dry. On my next trip into town I brought back the glass for the windows but the walls of the shed were never plastered. We hung tobacco paper. (a thick tarred paper used to wrap the dried and cured tobacco bales in) to separate our sleeping accommodation, from the living room. The kitchen was built at the side and wonders of wonders I had a wood stove to cook on. We now had a bathroom, with a bath, attached to the kitchen and a long drop not very far away. The only trouble was that once the rains set in one had to don a coat and gum boots to get to any of these facilities. But it was heaven for a while. It did not take me long to lay cinder paths between the shed and the kitchen and the bathroom.

We had hardly settled in our new "house" when a hurricane hit the district. Luckily we were on the edge of it but we spent the night under the beds as we were not sure if the roof would stay on. I'm afraid that my faith in my husband, as a provider of safe accommodation, had received a rather large crack. I lay on top of Gavin in order to protect his body with mine. As I lay there petrified my mind railed against John.

"Not only has he sold my home and separated me from my children but he now endangers our lives" I thought.

When the lightning flashed I could see the tall thin trees around the shed bending right over to touch the ground.

The noise of the wind and the thunder was deafening. The storm raged all night and in the morning when we crawled out from under the beds John stood at the door of the shed and surveyed the devastation of broken branches and uprooted trees.

"Well we got over that one alright!" he announced.

My answer was not repeatable as I stomped off to inspect the damage that had been done to my garden. John never knew how near I was to leaving him at that time. To him it was just another adventure.

As soon as we were able, we hurried over to our neighbors to see if all had escaped injury. Des and Helen had been lucky in that a large tree growing beside the house had crashed onto their veranda but no one had been hurt. Several barn roofs had been blown off and the roads were strewn with uprooted trees and branches. The hurricane had cut a swathe through the bush of several hundred feet destroying all in its path, but there were no human injuries.

John had started planting out the small tobacco plants into the field as soon as the first rain had fallen. The work force needed constant supervision and he was out in the field from sun up until dusk. I had had the honor of planting the first plant. However there were times when he could not stand guard over the labor and I took my turn at supervision. On these occasions Gavin came with me to the field and spent the day playing with the small African children who had accompanied their mothers to work. He became very good at talking the local dialect.

I started the twice a week transporting of building materials and fertilizer etc. The day began at about four in the morning when I set out. I usually arrived in Lusaka in time for a late breakfast. Then I loaded up the truck and started on the return trip late in the afternoon, arriving home well after sunset. Sometimes the trip required an overnight stay in Lusaka in which case I stayed with a friend, usually Jim and Joan at this time, so that I could see the girls. On these occasions I proudly took a box of my vegetables in with me.

I worried constantly about Gavin being left in the charge of the cook when I was away as John complained.

"He can't come with me! I can't keep my eyes on him while I'm supervising the laborers.

Gavin was only a very little boy after all but had been very well behaved when I had him in the fields. I did wonder why other fathers in the block managed to take their young sons to work with them on occasions. It seemed to me that this would be an excellent time for John to bond with his only son but it was not to be and the chance was lost for all time.

It was not long until Lore and Debby were at home for the Christmas holidays. Lore would start boarding school, at the convent in Kabwe towards the end of January and I would teach Debra at home with the aid of School on the Air. This excellent service was run by the Rhodesian Education Department for outlying farms. Lessons were posted but the twice weekly broadcasts were a great help. It was run on the same lines as the Australian system but of course we had no two way radio. Although I was not a Rhodesian resident they had generously agreed to let us join the school.

During these first holidays the girls took to swimming in the pits that had been dug to extract the clay for the bricks and had filled with rain water. Gavin took his first lessons in swimming there. One day coming unseen by the girls, I watched as Lore enticed Debby into the water.

"Come on Deb" she said. "It's quite deep,"

Unfortunately Debby did not realize that Lore was kneeling on the bottom of the pit. Debby showing off her new dive, plunged into the murky water only to come up with her hair stuck to her head with clay and her mouth and eyes filled with the yellow muck. Lore of course thought this was hilarious. Not so for poor Deb!

The only telephone in the district was at the farm of Joan and Viv some ten miles distance. We only used this phone in cases of emergency and it often took all morning to make a call to Lusaka. There was only one line to the area and the operators were to say the least inexperienced. It was a very frustrating and long winded task to get a message through. Joan kept open house for these times and their farm became the district meeting place. They had been on their farm for a few years already and were well established. Their house was unique in that it was built in several sections joined together at different angles. About four feet of brick work supported half a very large tank that formed the roof. It made a comfortable room if somewhat hot. Joan and Viv had seven children. The last born were twin boys. When Joan had started an early labor, they had set out for Broken hill with Joan's sister–in–law, Avvy, but the twins were born somewhere along the road with Viv and Avvy acting as midwives. We became great friends and we spent many a very pleasant evening with them. Not far from Joan and Viv, Avvy and Nevil farmed. Nevil was Joan's brother and Avvy was an expert hairdresser. A very much needed and used art.

Another family that we became close to was Marney and Nella. They were an Afrikaans family with four children and started farming at the same time as we did. Nella was an expert in using local produce, a trait inherited from her forbears, and she taught me many a useful recipe. All their children were at boarding school in South Africa.

Sensibly Marney had built a reasonable, temporary house when they first came onto their farm and they remained warm and dry during that first rainy season!

John Dendy Young and his wife farmed behind us. They had been there several years and John had done amazingly well. He owned a small plane as did another farmer a few miles away. John was very generous with transport in an emergency but we were all very careful not to take advantage of him.

New farmers arrived on the scheme after we did and we followed the district tradition by welcoming them with boxes of vegetables or whatever produce we had to hand.

On one occasion whilst visiting a very young couple, we were offered tea which we accepted. We waited while making small talk and waited. After some considerable time we got up to leave just as the tea arrived. The young couple only had one cup and had sent to the next farm to borrow some more.

Most of the families in the new part of the block had children. The older children went to boarding school and mothers taught the ones that were too young to go away. During the school holidays there was much coming and going between the farms and the children formed many friendships.

Fifty miles away to the north was the farmer's social club. Here we all met for various functions and during the school holidays there was always some entertainment laid on specifically for the children. At the Christmas party Father Christmas descended by parachute until one year he broke his leg in a bad landing. He came from the Copperbelt and his plane landed in front of the club house. It was difficult to explain to Gavin, that although in books, Father Christmas always arrived by reindeer and sledge, in the snow, at Mkushi he had to resort to parachute between the rain showers!

Debby, of course knew all about Father Christmas and listened with a very superior air.

At other times swimming galas and sports days were organized and at least once a holiday there was a film.

Paddy Barrett farmed several miles to the north of us. He was divorced and his three children often came for the holidays. The two oldest were girls a little older than Lore and Debby and the youngest, a boy, was about two years older than Gavin.

I think Paddy missed his family very much and was lonely. His elderly mother came to live with him but the arrangement was not a happy one. He would often come down to our farm and spend the day. I was sorry for his mother whom he never brought with him. It must have been a very lonely life for her as she did not drive and was therefore more or less marooned on the farm

Our farming block was situated between the Lunseem and Mkushi rivers and at their confluence the Mita Hills dam had been constructed to serve a copper mine, that due to the political situation, never was developed. This dam was a favorite place during the slack season for picnics.

Paddy owned a motor boat and we all learnt to water ski behind it. It must be admitted that the thought of crocodiles was never very far from my mind, but the dam had no swampy surrounds such as are inhabited by crocs. Eventually, however, one was shot there.

"It must have come overland as they are known to do" was generally believed and surprisingly we continued to swim there.

The noise of the motor boat kept any wild life away but the birds were wonderful. Several families of blue jays lived in the vicinity and their vivid blue colors caught the sunlight as they skimmed over the water. Kingfishers also added their bright plumage to the scene, and there was always the call of the wild doves, and the haunting cry of the fish eagle. On any tree that hung over the water, colonies of weaver birds fluttered and built their nests in close communities. They kept up such chattering and twittering that the whole tree appeared to be alive.

However, tragically one of the younger farmers from the north of the block killed himself while speed boating when his craft hit a submerged rock. It was a great blow to this small community. All the Europeans from the block attended his funeral in Kabwe. His wife found it impossible to carry on the farm without a man to keep discipline in the labor force, and was forced to leave the district. Mkushi was no place for a woman on her own on an isolated farm.

A favorite trip, during the dry season, when work on the farm was carried on at a slow pace, was to the leper colony called Fuwila Mission in the Luangwa valley about 70 miles from us, and 2000 feet lower in altitude. The road was only a dirt track and it was necessary to go by truck or jeep. We tried to make this an annual outing, taking old clothes and anything that we thought might be or some use to the nuns and priest who ran the mission.

As we came to the edge of the escarpment the terrain changed drastically. Whereas we farmed in rolling country, broken by the odd river, ridge, and outcrop of rocks the road now skirted steep sided hills and valleys. The trees became thicker and more bushy with lianas adorning the branches. Tree ferns grew in the clefts where small springs erupted from the rocks. Troops of baboons sent their barking calls echoing through the air and at times the troop scampered across the road in front of the truck, babies clinging to the under side of their mother's body, and the patriarch bringing up the rear while guarding any stragglers.

On the valley floor the bush reverted to mpani scrub except where the course of a stream or river was marked by thicker vegetation.

Fuwila is a Church of England mission and at that time it was staffed by two elderly nuns and one priest. The leper inmates varied from 40 to 50 in number. Unless in the last stages of the disease the patients lived in separate huts usually with their families that were built in a semicircle and white washed. All the ground around was swept clean.

The hospital was a long low building with a thatch roof for coolness and long verandas that were gauzed in to exclude mosquitoes. It supplied the needs of extreme cases. Being so low in altitude the heat here was more intense than on the plateau where we lived, but crops grew at such a rate that the mission was more or less self supporting. Everything was spotlessly clean and we were always welcomed by the patients and staff. The nuns made a great fuss of the children and plied them with cakes and sweets but what they wanted most was to talk and to catch up on any news. John usually went off with the priest to discuss some farming topic. It was expected of me that I would make a tour of the hospital and surrounding huts and talk to the various patients some of whom were hideously deformed and had been there for years. They greeted me as if I was an old friend.

Lazarus was one of these patients. He had been renamed by the Nuns when he was baptized a Christian possibly because they could not pronounce his African name. He was an old man now and in an advanced stage of the disease. His family had all died or disappeared back into the bush and he was alone.

Most of his toes were missing and he only had three fingers on one hand but his face had borne the worst ravages. His lips were non–existent and he only had a very large gaping hole where his mouth used to be. It was impossible to tell if Lazarus was smiling or not. Where once he had worn the tribal copper ear rings with pride there were now no lobes. His dry skin was covered with patches of pink nodules. But lazarus appeared to be always happy and spent his days helping the nuns with their work.

In the cool of the afternoon we sat with the nuns and the priest under the shady mufti trees and listened to them reminiscing about their homes so far away. They rarely left Africa.

My thoughts often return to the brave people who run these far away missions whatever their denomination, because their lives are hard and often very, very lonely

While traveling through the bush on these occasions we kept a sharp lookout for game. It was usually on the return trip as evening drew in that we were fortunate to spot the odd elephant or giraffe. Antelope were quite common and we often stopped to watch the antics of a herd of zebra. They appear to be such bad tempered animals, always kicking and chasing each other. However I cannot recall seeing any lions or predatory animals, who must have been there but were well camouflaged.

We were very wary of watching herds of elephants as these animals were not used to trucks. However on one occasion whilst passing along the Luangwa river we did stop to watch a small herd with several babies playing at the waters edge. It was great to see them sliding down the muddy bank, splashing and squirting each other with their trunks. The adults kept a sharp lookout that the youngsters did not come to any harm and even once called the babies out of the water when a hippo came too near for comfort.

The Luangwa River is home to many herds of hippo and we watched them wallowing in the shallows. They are really ungainly beasts but can move with surprising speed if aggravated. Discretion is definitely the better part of valor when a hippo decides that one is trespassing on its territory. A great attraction for me is the call of the big black and white fish eagle that can be found by any stretch of water. They perch on the dead branches of trees overhanging the river silhouetted against the sky, and their lonely cry sums up the vast reaches of this varied and magnificent land.

As the sun started to sink we were forced to leave the scene as we still had many miles to go before reaching home.

CHAPTER 15

Animals have always formed a very important part of my life and an odd assortment have marched with me through the years. In my childhood, besides the dogs and cats there were the usual rabbits, guinea pigs, and at one time a warthog. So when, in the first couple of months, on the farm John bought home a two day old duiker (species of antelope) it was received with warm affection. On returning from town, that night, John had seen, in the headlights of the truck, an African carrying the baby, upended by his four feet.

"What have you got there?" asked John. "Nyama" (meat) the African answered.

John looked at the baby duiker, his head lolling just above the ground and his dark eyes, fringed by long black lashes, wide open with fright. How could anyone resist the sight, let alone John, to whom all wild life was more or less sacred? John haggled and bargained with the African for 10 minutes and eventually after paying the princely sum of about 50p. our family was increased by one baby duiker.

In Zambia, spring arrives in September, and this is the time when the duikers give birth to their young. The mother will leave the baby concealed in the long grass when she goes to feed in the late evening and the African must have stumbled upon him on his way through the bush.

When John arrived home he said

"Look Roni, I've got a present for you". and he showed me the duiker that was lying docilely on the truck seat beside him.

"O! You poor baby", I exclaimed when John handed him to me and explained how he had purchased him.

A bed in a box was quickly prepared and one of the dogs, Boots, staked an instant claim to the baby and became a surrogate mother. Duikers are notoriously hard to rear as the mother's milk is difficult to replace, but this one, with persistent help from Boots survived. Boots guarded him, muzzled and cleaned him constantly

Gavin, at that time spent most of his days singing Yankee Doodle and when asked what to name the new addition he immediately said " Doodle". And so Doodle he became.

Doodle was never locked up. When he graduated from his cardboard box, he roamed the farmstead at will and when old enough made his sleeping place on an anthill at the rear of the shed where we were then living. He was never far from the children or dogs and joined in the rough and tumble with alacrity. In the early morning as soon as the big shed doors were opened, he would clip–clop over the wooden floor and jump straight onto my bed, and proceed to give me a very wet greeting with his rough pink tongue.

He had very large expressive brown eyes framed by long dark eyelashes. His coat was a golden brown and it blended in with the grass perfectly, so that sometimes he was difficult to find if he decided to play hide and seek. The underside of his stumpy tail was white but his sharp little hooves were a shiny black. When fully grown he stood at about two and a half feet tall.

In the heat of the day, when the haze shimmered on the horizon and threw mirages of cool lakes onto the golden grass, the dogs collapsed into any available shade. All work stopped for a few hours while animals and humans alike waited for the usual cloud build up or a slight breeze to alleviate the intense heat.

At this time, if the mood possessed him, Doodle would nudge and gird the dogs until they awoke. He would then take off down the long vlei in front of the shed with the dogs in hot pursuit. We would listen to their frantic barking disappearing into the distance and smile knowingly at each other.

Eventually Doodle would tip–tap back into the shed looking bright and breezy and very innocent. In an hour or so the exhausted dogs would straggle home to flop down by the water trough. This was his favorite game and the dogs never learnt that they could not catch him.

Doodle had a passion for green tomatoes and although banned from the vegetable garden he always managed to find a way in. He could demolish a bed of plants in minutes. When I found him standing in a crushed bed with his cheeks bulging with the green fruit, I would shout at him

"Doodle get out of that bed"

and I would dive and try to catch him. He would look up at me with his big innocent eyes and stay just out of my reach. It was usually Pieman who came to save him from my wrath.

The ant hill at the back of the shed, where Doodle had elected to make his sleeping quarters, was very high and had several tall trees growing on it. Because of the steep sides it was ideal for the monkey rope that John had erected for the children. They and their friends spent many a happy hour playing there, swinging and doing acrobatics on the long rope.

One day, one of the girls came to me.

"There is little man watching us from the grass on the side of the ant hill," she said.

It was all too easy to put this down to an overactive imagination but something prompted me to investigate the appearance of this strange creature. To my horror I discovered two very large snakes emerging from their hole in the ant hill. Doodle had no objection to the reptiles and sniffed around them. Well he had been sharing the same bedroom! Not so with me! I'm afraid I'm not brave enough to turn my back and let them go on their way especially as the children played in this place. John was ill with what I thought to be malaria at that time and so it was no use appealing to him for help.

We never kept a fire arm on our farm. Neither John nor I could tolerate any hunting of wild animals and were of the opinion that most deaths through firearms were caused by accident. But there were some occasions when one had to resort to desperate measures and this was one of them.

Having corralled all the children and dogs I got into the truck and hurried over to a Marney to beg for help. He returned with me bringing his rifle, but by this time Pieman had already set fire to the hole into which the snakes had retreated and had extracted them. They lay on the ground writhing in agony with half their skin burnt off. Pieman stood over them watching, leaning on his stick, obviously pleased with his action and quite impervious to the suffering of the reptiles. But I could not bear to see any creature suffer in such a way and Marney dispatched them with alacrity at my request.

I never did discover the identity of these reptiles and the years have dimmed the picture of their markings but they were as I recall, 8 and ten feet long respectively.

This incident, on reflection, taught me that wild creatures can and do live in perfect harmony. Doodle was obviously happy in their company.

Doodle grew very quickly and in no time, or so it seemed, the two little bumps on the top of his head started to develop into horns. His little hoofs were very sharp and he was well aware as to how to use them. Gavin and Doodle were inseparable and together with Boots, the other dogs, and at one time a lamb, roamed the farm buildings and gardens at will usually in Indian file.

However Doodle was reluctant to rest at any time and in order to goad Gavin into action he would butt the boy with his heed or jump on him with his little legs stiff and his sharp hoofs pointed.

We were obviously faced with a serious problem. This situation could not continue as Doodle's horns would be able to inflict a serious wound on Gavin in the future, however innocent his butting was at that time. Duikers are notoriously vicious when in rut, and stags are known to kill each other at these times. If we took Doodle to some far off part of the bush he would be too trusting and would soon fall prey to either human or animal. If we dehorned him and he eventually went in search of a mate, as was natural, he would be in the same unprotected state, although Gavin would be safe from his sharp horns. To lock him up was unthinkable

Eventually we heard of a wild life park that promised that they could protect him whilst giving him the necessary freedom. He would, in time, be given his own herd of females and would have his own paddock. This seemed an ideal solution to the problem although we would be heart broken to lose him.

So sadly the whole family, including Doodle, climbed into the truck and made the journey to the Kafue Game Park. All had been explained to the children but this did not soften the parting.

Gavin and Doodle sat huddled together in the back of the truck for the whole journey. I'm sure Doodle knew that we were to abandon him. It was like leaving a child.

"I won't cry if Doodle hurts me with his horns" Gavin cried.

But with tears rolling down my cheeks I loosened Gavin's fingers from around Doodle's neck and with a final hug I handed him over to the Game Keeper. I then took my son into my arms and we cried together until his sobs had subsided and he fell asleep worn out with the emotion. When my eyes had cleared enough we drove home all very subdued and sad.

Several months later we returned to the game park and trekked to the paddock where Doodle had set up home with his harem. He did not respond to our calls and seemed anxious to keep his new family from our intrusion. I could not help the tug at my heartstrings as we left for the last time. It would have been nice if Doodle had answered to our calls, but perhaps it was all for the best as he had obviously returned to the wild.

The baby turkeys that I had so lovingly carried on my lap during my first journey to the farm, grew and prospered. When they were old enough they had free range over the farm where they bred and if we lost many to the compound or predators we had enough for our own consumption. One of the original six grew up to be a magnificent tom who ruled the roost. He took a wild delight in chasing Debby and Gavin if they came upon him unawares. It was quite frightening for them when this bird, called Tom, came at them with his tail spread out and his wing feathers stiffly raking the ground with a peculiar hissing sound. His head would be lowered for striking but every few minutes he would raise it and give his shout of "Gobble, gobble"

While we were in the shed, the loo was situated behind the brick bathroom, but was constructed of grass with a curved wall instead of a door. This would be demolished when we moved into a house and so was not worth a brick construction.

During the day, when the children were doing their lessons in the shed and they needed to take a trip to the loo, they would look out the door to see that Tom was not in the vicinity, and then together make a mad dash for the outhouse. But Tom always knew where they were and lay in ambush. He always allowed them out of the shed but when they wanted to return he would be standing proud at the opening to the loo and in response to loud wails of

"Mummy, Tom wont let us out"

. I would have to run to their rescue and escort them back to the shed after bribing him away with some bread or grain. I received many a peck on my legs from this bird!

In order to have fresh eggs and meat I bought day–old chicks, 50 to 100 at a time about twice a year. These took a great deal of time to rear but were invaluable both for our own use and for sale. Eventually I bought a second hand incubator and incubated our own eggs. To do this I was very selective in what cocks escaped the pot as these provided my breeding stock. And so the more aggressive and bigger the bird, the safer he was. But my best cock developed a dislike for anything in skirts and if I entered the henhouse in one he would fly at me. Strangely if I was wearing trousers I escaped his wild attention. I only discovered this fact after having been trapped in the henhouse on several occasions and receiving numerous wounds to my legs. Perhaps the lesson is to dress for the occasion!

The worst part of this situation was that after I had been forced to beat a hasty, undignified and humiliating retreat he would retire to the top of the henhouse, flap his wings and crow! No amount of dire threats of the pot had any effect on him at all.

My first attempt at the incubator was with only six eggs and out of these I managed to rear two chicks. I did improve in time but these two became house pets and were named by the children as Henny Penny and Cocky Lokky. At that stage my children were not renowned for their originality!

Henny Penny was the more house trained of the two and to John went the honor of her first egg which was laid in his jersey on the couch. However this was much later when we were finally in a house.

Ant hills are a scourge in Central Africa, and Zambia has it's fair share of them. These are complex structures, built by termites, and can be as large as 2.5 meters in height and

10.20 meters in diameter. How deep they penetrate the earth depends on the age and population of the community. During the rainy season swarms of these ants develop wings and literally erupt from the ant hill. These are mating rituals and eventually the insects fall to earth and drop their wings. Some African tribes collect them for food and they form a reserve of protein. However, there are times when the complete ant community decides to move. On these occasions the ordinary workers develop into very large soldier ants.

One night, during the school holidays, and when we had already moved into our house, we returned from the club fairly late. The children fell asleep almost immediately and John and I were not far behind. John was woken by something crawling over him which persisted in spite of being brushed away. He lit the candle and discovered that the wall next to his bed was alive with very large army ants. They had crawled over the windowsill and were determinedly eating their way through his blankets.

"Get up Roni" John called. "The place is alive with army ants"

As I staggered up from the bed and reached for the torch I saw that the floor was a moving carpet of the insects.

Our first concern was the children sleeping at the back of the house, but after a hasty scrutiny we were assured that they were safe for the time being as their rooms were securely screened.

Fortunately, there were torches to hand and we found our working shoes beside the kitchen door which we thankfully donned after brushing and pulling the horrible biting things from our legs. We thought that if we could manage to burn them as they were entering the house we would be able to turn their march aside. We managed to pull smoldering logs from the boiler at the rear of the house and set alight to some leafy wood. But in spite of jumping round like wild banshees with burning branches, this was to no avail. Then John remembered that there was a tin of insecticide and a stirrup pump in the back store.

"Bring the bucket and the pump" John called

And so dressed only in scanty night wear and work shoes we spent the next few hours spraying around the house, John holding the spray and me hauling the bucket and working the pump. The ants in the house sensed that they had been cut off from the main arm and slowly retreated. We were lucky that the moon was bright as I could not have managed the pump while holding onto a torch. Eventually, as the sun came up the main arm of the marchers swung away from the house and although exhausted we were able to mop up the stragglers.

The two chicks, Henny Penny and Cocky Lokky, that I had raised slept in the back store and had been attacked by the ants. All the flesh had been stripped from their legs and combs by the ants which we had to pull off by our finger nails leaving in places the bones exposed. I treated their wounds and they did survive. Perhaps this was why they became such pets.

In the early morning light we could see the route that the ants had taken from an ant hill at the side of the house and we were able to trace their passage by the corridors that they had built as they progressed and the trail of devastation that they left in their wake. It was a time to thank God for deliverance.

It was a long time before we were organized enough to invest in livestock to any extent but while we were still in the tractor shed we did buy in a small flock of sheep. They were only short haired scrub animals but provided a welcome change from poultry on the table. They were really more trouble than they were worth as they had to be herded, which meant employing a herdboy. They also had to be deticked once a week. As we did not have a dip this was done by a hand spray and I often wondered if the herdboy or myself did not receive more spray than the sheep. Because of their tendency to pick up all sorts of parasites they also had to be dosed regularly and had to be kept off the new grass that sprang up after the fires. If the herd did stray onto this kind of grass, their stomachs would blow up with an excess of some kind of acid and I was unable to save the animal.

At the beginning of this experiment we did not keep the ram separate as the herd was so small and lambing could be at any time of the year. The first lamb that was rejected by its mother was brought up on the bottle by Debby and she called her Merrylegs. Merrylegs eventually joined the children in their wanderings and brought up the rear of the parade of dogs and Doodle. It took me a long time to return her to the flock and to convince her that she really was a sheep.

At times, the families in our vicinity would club together and purchase a couple of weaners from the more established farmers to the north of the block. These cattle were always slaughtered there and transported down by truck. John on these occasions came into his own and did the carving up of the beasts.

Nella then became the sausage and boerewors (a very highly spiced Afrikaans sausage with coriander) queen. She spent many hours mincing the meat adding the special herbs and spices and then packing it into the sausage skins. This was all done on a hand mincer and the women all took turns at turning the handle of the mincer as it was arm breaking work.

John made a brine and several choice cuts were salted. The offal and skins were given to the labor force who much appreciated them.

A deep freeze, run on paraffin, was an essential household commodity and it was a relief to have it filled with our share of the meat. I often wondered how my mother had managed without fridges. I remember one meat safe that my father had built. It consisted of two lines of chicken wire fixed to a frame and charcoal packed between the wire. Water dripped down onto the wire and the evaporation kept the interior cool.

On several occasions I tried my hand at making bacon and ham. As pigs are not such large animals we usually bought one for ourselves or to share with one other neighbor. John dealt with the cleaning and cutting up of the animal and I undertook the salting. John had given me the recipe for the brine and I injected this into the meat every couple of inches with the aid of a hypodermic syringe from the snakebite kit. The joint was then put into a plastic bag filled with the brine, placed in the deep freeze for some time, and then hung up to dry. My ambition was to have a smoke house but the green bacon was very welcome.

At one time, we purchased two live pigs from a farmer who wanted to dispose of them quickly. This was unusual as the animals were usually slaughtered by the seller. However, as it was in the middle of the grading season, John had no time to slaughter and butcher them.

I prepared a sty for them in an old brick pit and they stayed there for some considerable time, until one day they broke out. For some reason they made a dash for the grading shed where the labor force was busy and burst through the door with Pieman and me in hot pursuit. They were obviously terrified and careered around leaving a trail of mud, upsetting tobacco bales, chasing the graders and generally causing mayhem. The African women, who were helping with the grading, screamed and grabbing their children all made for the door upsetting buckets of water and scattering tobacco leaves. As they could not all get through the door at one time they screamed all the louder thus exciting the pigs more. It was bedlam. Eventually, the pigs were corralled and subdued. The grading shed was returned to normal amidst much hilarity. Everyone was pointing at another and saying how ridiculous they looked and generally enjoying the memory of an episode that enlivened an otherwise boring day.

Pieman and I hastily repaired the sty after penning the pigs behind some tobacco bales, and carefully herded them back.

They went docilely enough but by the glint in their beady little eyes, they too had thoroughly enjoyed their brief spell of freedom.

CHAPTER 16

The tobacco seed beds were situated near the borehole for easy watering. They were also on the main road which bordered the reserve. There were no fences and the cattle from the reserve roamed freely. On two occasions in our first year they crossed the road and trampled our seedbeds. This meant that the seedbeds had to be resown and the program for the year was delayed quite drastically.

In order to stop the occurrence John decided to attend the court of the reigning Chief. To go by truck would take several hours over a very bad road, so on the advice of the foreman or 'Boss Boy' as they liked to be called, John decided to go by bicycle through the bush. He borrowed a bike and with the Boss Boy set out to attend the court. He had been told that it was 'Doozy, doozy' which meant not very far. However, the African does not judge distances like we do and the trip took John the best part of the day. As he labored along the paths news of his progress was always before him and whenever he came to a kraal or small collection of huts, there would be water and a dish of hard boiled eggs waiting for him. Such is the hospitality of the bush African that I don't think John ate another hard boiled egg for years.

In the council hut, which was a large thatched roofed construction with the sides open, John waited his turn to air his grievance. He was enthralled at the patience the Chief had whilst the various supplicants stated their cases. Everyone was given as much time as they required and the day dragged on and on. Eventually 'The case of the trampled seedbeds' came up and after lengthy debate the owner of the cattle was told to keep his beasts elsewhere, but in future years John would site the seedbeds further from the road. He came home that evening somewhat wiser in African Justice and a very tired man indeed.

Later that year John decided that we should make a courtesy call to the Chief and one Sunday we set off in the truck for a very long and uncomfortable drive. I was not in favor of this trip and was reluctant to accompany him. John was adamant that I attend and that if the women were segregated I was to go with them.

"None of this women's lib." He said.

The Chief was reputed to have been educated at Cambridge and I suspect that John expected some upper class residence. He really should have known better as he was not a new arrival in Africa.

Having been born and brought up here I understood the African a lot better than he did as it soon appeared, but I kept my counsel. After two hours of bone breaking travel we arrived at the village which was just a collection of grass huts. There was not a soul to be seen; even the children, who normally abounded at a kraal like this, were absent. All the doors of the huts were tightly closed.

A few scruffy chickens scratched in the bare earth. The usual tick–infested, and half starved dogs raised their uninterested heads to regard us and then slinked off into the shade.

A half empty drum stood by the still smoldering embers of a fire and around this the sand showed signs of many foot prints. An old bicycle stood at a crazy angle against one of the few trees that had been left standing in the area. Several boxes and broken chairs lay haphazardly strewn around.

When we finally found a young boy who was herding some goats he informed us, mostly by sign language that there had been a beer drinking session the night before and it had continued, as was the customs until sun up, with the result that the whole community was laid out in drunken stupor! John's temper was not improved by my laughter!

A few weeks passed. John received a message from the Chief that he would call at our farm on the following Sunday afternoon as a return visit. He would bring one or two members of his council with him.

I prepared tea, with cake and sandwiches, for the men, and then left John to entertain his guests while I took the children and went for a long walk.

Apparently the Chief was not satisfied with the 'tea' that I had provided and more or less demanded alcohol. There was none in the shed at that time, much to his disappointment.

As the Chief and his Councilors left the shed Tom, the turkey had to allay his curiosity and boldly walked around the departing guests. The Chief was intrigued by him and informed John that he would have some of these birds as a parting present.

John replied

"They don't belong to me but to my wife. You will have to ask her."

The Chief regarded John with a jaundiced eye. In his culture a woman never owned anything.

I'm quite sure that the Chief did get his turkeys in time as they had free range over the farm and were always disappearing, but I wonder if there would have been less theft from the farm later, if I had graciously consented to make a gift of the birds.

Lore started boarding school at the Convent in Kabwe, at the end of January. She did not enjoy it and although I saw her as often as I was allowed to, she did not settle in well. It tore at my heart each time I had to leave her in tears.

I started teaching Debby, on the days that I was not away in the truck and on those days when I was, she had set lessons to do. From the start it was not a very satisfactory situation as she really needed constant supervision.

We had not been on the farm for more than a year when the Government decided that no employer should dole out rations of food to their workforce but should raise the pay to compensate. This suited the majority of farmers very well as the weekly chore of handing out the rations was very time consuming. However as there was no shop within easy reach of our farm, it meant that one member of the laborer's family had to make a very long walk every time food supplies were needed.

And so John decided that I should open a farm store. Apart from the fact that I knew nothing about bookkeeping, or trading for that matter, I considered that what with the transporting, teaching the children, and running the house and garden and being a substitute farmer, I had enough to do. But John was adamant and so shop keeper I became on those days when I was not traveling to and from Lusaka.

A shop was built on the main road with very strong steel doors. The area around it was cleared leaving several shady trees. An Indian trader, Mr. Patel, in Kabwe, guided me through the stocking of it. This took the remainder of the capital that we had managed to save from the sale of our house in Lusaka but in the main it proved to be a very profitable enterprise once I understood the basic pricing and costing.

The Africans who came to the store, used the occasion for social gathering and would sit in the shade of the surrounding trees, gossiping and generally exchanging the district news. The women in their bright dresses with contrasting head scarves and long, dangling, beaded ear rings resembled a flock of gaily colored birds. Each woman had a baby strapped to her back and often two or three children played around her feet in the sand. She had probably walked several miles carrying a bundle on her head and her latest baby on her back. She walked bare footed and held her shoes in her hand to save them. When she entered the store they would be on her feet.

A healthy African baby is beautiful. He has very large solemn, brown eyes and because he is never far from his mother is generally a happy child. His mother carries him on her back, held on by a sling made from a towel or piece of material. Food is on demand whilst he is being breast fed and as he grows older the breast is often offered as a comforter until he has outgrown it. I never saw an African child smacked.

The children have very few or no toys except those made by themselves such as reed whistles. They start work at a very early age, the girls carrying water and helping with the younger children and the boys herding the cattle or goats.

Visit any African village and their hospitality knows no bounds but as a people they are extremely gullible and highly volatile.

Because of my clinic I got to know many of the children very well and watched them grow and develop in character. With many I made friends but there was always a barrier which neither side overstepped.

I often wished that I understood their local dialect. I did speak a Chilapalapa, or Kitchen Kaffir, as it was called, and could make myself understood but was sadly lacking in being able to understand the laughter and conversations (many at my expense) that went on outside the store.

I stocked a variety of goods from bicycle spares to baby's napkins. The bolts of brightly colored material were sold by the yard and were then taken to another store, some miles down the road, and made up into the style that the women desired. So eventually I purchased an old treadle sewing machine and employed a tailor. I found some old fashion books on one of my trips to town and some blown up pictures of different dresses which I pinned up round the store. And we became the fashion house of the district!

But I found serving behind the counter very tedious. An African would ask for a box of matches. The transaction would be completed and change given. Then he, or she would request a candle and the whole process would be repeated until the weeks shopping was finished.

I set up a desk in the store for Debby to do her lessons while I was there, and on the days when I was transport riding she stayed with Gavin in the shed.

The teaching did not progress very well as without supervision the lessons were done very hurriedly or not at all. There was many a shouting and crying match when I discovered that the set lesson had not been carried out to my satisfaction. John considered that the teaching was women's work and would take no part in it.

I also worried constantly when I was away that the children were not getting the care needed and were left in the charge of the cook as John spent his days out in the fields. Another worry was the fact that the estate car had gracefully given up the ghost, and as no spares were available in the country had been retired. This meant that when either of us were away in the truck there was no transport on the farm.

Because of the late start we barely made enough money from our first tobacco crop to cover the costs of planting. But we did have 20 acres of maize that we were to keep for rations for the labor.

The maize was left standing in the fields until dry and then reaped by hand. It was then put through a mill when required and made into meal.

The stalks were left in the ground until we had enough time to attend to them which this year would be later than ideal.

John decided, when the crop had been reaped and time was running short, to knock them down and then burn them off so that the field could be replanted. In order to flatten the plants, which had grown to well over six feet, and get a clean burn, he would use both the tractors. We had at that time a small Ferguson and a much larger John Deer tractor. A heavy chain was attached at each end to the rear of both tractors and the idea was that the tractors would progress together over the field pulling the chain between them and so flattening the maize. John spent a long time explaining the method to the two drivers and stressing that they must keep watching each other, and keep the a speed.

The senior tractor driver, called Tarzan, had come out from Lusaka with us and was accompanied by a locally recruited driver called Sixpence.

173

At a given signal from John, both tractors revved up and proceeded slowly. John walked backwards in front of them to ensure that they kept pace with each other. All went well until Tarzan's tractor came upon an ant hill and therefore fell behind. Sixpence ignored the loud shouts from John and continued if at anything a faster rate. John now ran frantically backwards, stumbling over the stalks, while shouting and waving at the oblivious Sixpence. He watched in horror as the tractor on which Tarzan was precariously perched slowly turned over. Tarzan jumped clear and eventually Sixpence felt the strain on his tractor and stopped. It was a very expensive event but watching the tableau from the side of the field I could not contain my laughter. The whole episode seemed to happen in slow motion.

During his frantic backwards sprint, over the field, John had come into contact with a rock or branch and badly cut his shin. When we finally reached the shed I cleaned away the dried blood and as usual washed the wound with permanganate before strapping on a dressing.

That evening as there was little or no breeze we went back to the mealie field accompanied by the children and the dogs and set fire to the dry mealie stalks.

Because of the danger of bush fires guards of several feet of cleared bush had been made around the field. We watched the fire burn down, and as as there was no wind to fan any ashes into flame, we felt sure, that if not completely out the fire would not spread too far.

Later that night when I fed the dogs one, Patch, was missing. Although I called he didn't come and I concluded that he had gone off hunting.

After a hectic day on the farm that usually started with the sunrise we always went to bed early. As soon as the lamps were out and their distinctive hum silenced, I heard a dog howling in the distance. I realized that it must be Patch who was probably caught in a snare that the Africans set to catch game.

The thought of the fire we had set and the howling of the dog came together in a flash. Without further thought, and dressed only in my pajamas and sandals I was out of the shed and running through the bush in the dark, towards the mealie field. John in hot pursuit shouted at me not to be such a fool.

I found Patch with the fire within a couple of feet of his cowering body and his leg firmly held in a snare. It did not take us long to release him and we then carried him home. All the way back John lectured me on the irresponsible way I had run out.

As we came towards the shed we could see that most of our labor force were standing around the big double doors with Debby and Gavin in front of them screaming their heads off. Having seen their Father and me run out of the shed and not knowing what was the matter they had at first shouted and then started crying. The Africans had heard them and all congregated in front of the shed.

Eventually all was restored to normal. Patch was fed, the labor force retired to the compound, Debby and Gavin assured that we would not leave them alone and we all went to a well earned rest.

However, John's leg, in spite of my tender care would not heal. It kept breaking out and suppurating, and complete rest was impossible as the new season had started and the planting had to continue.

Lore came home from school for the Christmas holidays and there was a respite from teaching. The rains set in turning the roads into streams and some of the rivers burst their banks

On the morning of Christmas Eve John was very ill. He was running a high temperature and was delirious. I was in a terrible dilemma. There was no one to turn to for advice and I was not sure of the reason for John's high temperature. Whenever John had had a high temperature in the past, he always became delirious but this knowledge did not dispel my anxiety

We always took malaria preventative tablets and yet John's symptoms were very like those of malaria. On the other hand, the wound on his leg had once again broken out and his leg was very inflamed. If it was malaria and I had put him in the truck and taken him to town I might have ruptured his spleen traveling over the rough roads. In any case one of the rivers had overflowed a bridge so it was impossible to get to town.

Alternatively if it was the infection in his leg that was causing the fever he needed more than the poultices that I had been applying.

I had heard of a farmer's wife at the top of the block who ran a clinic under license and would have some penicillin, which could halt the infection in his leg.

I turned the problem over in my mind all morning. John was alternately sweating and shivering and I battled to keep his temperature down by sponging him. The kitchen was festooned with sheets I had removed from his bed and hung out to dry. There was not a dry piece of linen in the house.

Eventually I made up my mind and leaving Lore in charge I traveled up to the top of the block in the truck. It was raining heavily and the trip was a series of skids and slips and I worried constantly that if I broke down or got caught in the mud my return would be seriously delayed and Lore would not be able to deal with the situation.

But my Guardian Angel was with me that night. I begged the nurse for the penicillin and returning home with it late in the evening, at once gave John an injection. At the same time I stepped up the malaria tablets.

Christmas Eve and the children and I sat around a white painted twig festooned with streamers, whispering Christmas carols while on the other side of the paper partition John raved and sweated.

In the morning after a very long night there appeared to be no change in John's condition, and I continued with the penicillin and malaria tablets. The rain had stopped and Christmas Day dawned bright and clear. The children opened their presents but were subdued and frightened. At about 11 o'clock I packed up the turkey dinner into baskets and sent my three children across the bush to Marney and Nella. It says a lot for their courage that with Lore to lead them they set off without a backward look. I of course worried until Marney brought them home that evening. There had been no one to send with them as the Africans had been issued with beer for Christmas and the whole compound was comatose.

However in answer to my prayers John's fever broke that afternoon and although he was weak for several days he was able to wish the children a Happy Christmas and give them each a kiss. We never did discover if it was malaria or his leg that had caused the fever.

CHAPTER 17

Besides the original twenty acres of cleared land that was already on the farm when we arrived, John had managed to clear a further twenty acres the first year, on which he had planted maize. Tobacco is grown on virgin soil and can support a second crop after which the land is used for maize or other crops depending on the rotation plan. Maize can be grown on the same land for up to three years when, there must be a change of crop or the yield will deteriorate.

In the second year John had cleared a further twenty acres, bringing our tobacco crop to 40 acres. Now we desperately needed more cleared land in order to fill the terms of our contract and to meet our quota of tobacco. After weighing up the pros and cons, John decided to bring in a contractor who would stump a large area of land with bulldozers. The alternative was to clear it with our own laborers, a long and costly process. It seemed the sensible thing to do as it would solve the yearly problem of finding enough labor to do the job.

The ridge in front of the site intended for our house was chosen. Although it had many beautiful trees on it, there would be easy access to the farm buildings where the tobacco would be cured in the new barns that were nearly complete.

Tobacco is best grown on gentle slopes as it does not favor 'wet feet'. To prevent the soil being washed away in the heavy rains, contour ridges would have to be constructed. The land would then be ridged and fertilized ready for planting as required. The wood from the felled trees would provide fuel for the barns for several years if we could prevent it all being eaten by white ants.

John was very insistent that the fields should have a thick border of trees around them, which would make the fireguards difficult to maintain but would help the resident wild life. We had on several occasions seen a herd of sable grazing in the vleis, their magnificent horns silhouetted against the evening skyline, and we were very keen that they remain in the vicinity. There were also smaller buck like Doodle and of course the ever present baboons who we were sure would wreck havoc with the maize in time.

On the first day of the land clearing, I walked over, with the children to watch. As the bull dozers knocked over the trees, the hyraxes or bush babies (Similar to a squirrel but with large brown eyes) were thrown from their perches. They are nocturnal and were all asleep when they were so rudely woken. They cried like babies as they fell from the trees and the Africans set upon them with clubs. They would later provide a meal for their families. But I found that I could not watch. Besides the killing of the bush babies the sight of those magnificent trees crashing down was too much for me.

The development of the farm went ahead in leaps and bounds and we started to plan for the building of our house. As we would have to rely on the same African builders who had constructed the barns, and who were not master builders by any stretch of the imagination, the design would be kept as simple as we could. Basically it would have three long walls, the center one being the tallest so that the roof would have a hip on it. The space beneath would be divided into the rooms that we required and the front would have the long veranda with a half wall for seating. There would be very large windows in all the rooms to catch any breeze, but these would all have screens on them to prevent the mosquitoes and flies etc from coming in. The large sitting room was to have a fireplace as the winter evenings can become very cool to those of us who were used to the heat of the days. This proved to be very difficult and John made the builders rebuild the fireplace three times before he was satisfied with it.

John and I had several friendly arguments on the interior design. The dining room was a rather small room and we could not agree if it should have windows only or french doors with windows either side. When the house was complete we discovered that we had forgotten the windows altogether and it only had french doors, which made it uncomfortable on hot evenings as they could not be gauzed in and therefore had to be shut to keep out the insects that were drawn in by the light. It took several months to construct the house as the builders were always being taken away for some other job on the farm buildings.

Another factor in the delay was the political situation. Imported goods became very difficult to find and it became necessary to improvise on many things.

Zambia is a land locked country. The only railway at that time was that which came up across the Victoria Falls from Rhodesia. The main road access followed the railway line or crossed the Zambezi valley at Chirundu. From Lusaka it continued north to the Copper Belt. Some sixty miles north of Kabwe a very rough, untarred road branched off from the main road to the Copper Belt, at Kapiri Mposhi and progressed up through the northern province of Zambia, across the wide expanse of Tanzania, finally terminating at Dar es Salaam on the coast of the Indian Ocean. . We had to travel many miles on this road to reach the turn off to our farming block. Kapiri Mposhi, where there was a pub, became a staging post before finishing the long trip home from from Lusaka or Kabwe.

I often paused on my homeward journey here but because the rest of my trip would require all my concentration I rationed myself to one brandy. Not so the young rakes from the block and on many occasions an impromptu party developed which if I was present I joined with pleasure.

On one occasion I had stopped at the pub and enjoyed a drink with Fred, Allan and Bill, three young bachelors from the block who farmed on adjoining farms. As was the custom, when someone was making the trip into town people would ask for a lift in. It was much more pleasant to travel with others than by oneself. So these three had spent a busy day in Lusaka and on returning had called into the Kapiri Mposhi pub. There they imbibed rather more than was advisable and on returning to the truck discovered that it would not start. Obligingly Allan and Bill alighted and started to push the truck. Imagine their dismay when as the truck fired and roared off Fred lent from the cab.

"Thanks a million" he called as the truck disappeared in a cloud of dust.

Allan and Bill were left standing on the road with their mouths hanging open.

"Well he probably wasn't in a fit state to drive anyway" as Allan remarked to Bill.

The two did return to their farms but only the next day in another neighbor's car. When confronted with this gross betrayal Fred swore that he could not remember anything. The three did remain firm friends but one wonders how the odds were eventually evened.

However, the change in the country was almost tangible. Whereas in the past as I drove the truck down the dusty roads at certain places I would wave and receive answering cheers. I often stopped the truck on my homeward journey and bought the wild mushrooms or pumpkins that the Africans sold at the road side. We would exchange news of the weather and crops after we had completed our bargaining and sometimes exchanged a joke or two, which was difficult as I was not very good at the local tongue.

Now the atmosphere was more somber and I no longer received any answering wave. Nor did I stop now to buy the produce offered at the side of the road.

The fact that I was only too well aware of the events that had caused this change in attitude in the rural Africans did little to help restore my confidence.

The staple food of the African in Central Africa, is maize, which if not eaten off the cob is ground down to make a meal which is then boiled and eaten as a stiff porridge, generally with a vegetable which he calls relish. The rural African, at that time only grew enough maize for his own consumption as food or made into beer. He did not stump out his lands. The trees were cut down just above ground level and then when the first rains had fallen and softened the ground the whole family dug over the area between the trees stumps and planted the maize. The women then took over the cultivation of the 'fields'.

In this manner the rural African usually provides enough for his immediate needs. In a bad year, if the rains came late, or if there was a drought, the family faced a very serious possibility of starvation unless they could find the money to buy in food.

However, those who had no land found food becoming very scarce with the departure of the European commercial farmer who provided most of the maize for the town population, and the restriction of imports of maize from the south.

One year some well meaning charity in England purchased and donated to numerous African farmers, farming implements. These consisted of a tractor pulling trailer on top of which was a plough, disc harrow and a drum of diesel. Whenever I traveled on the main road, I saw these tractors going out to some obscure and distant part of the country. How many there were I have no idea, but judging from the number that came up the 'Great North Road', I should think that the numbers were in their thousands rather than the hundreds. It was in many ways an unfortunate occurrence as when the tractor broke down, or had a puncture, or ruptured the sump on a tree stump, there was no one available to help the farmer put things to rights again. Then his whole enterprise fell apart and he became understandably bitter. He looked for someone to vent his frustration on and who better than the European farmer who was, from all accounts, succeeding where he had failed.

Much the same situation was occurring in the towns. Before Independence the rival African political parties had promised their followers that if they were elected all would have European houses and cars etc. Of course this did not materialize. Many rural Africans flocked into the towns to take part in this free bonanza and shanty towns sprang up on the outskirts of the towns and cities. There was no work to be found and security deteriorated at an alarming speed.

I could no longer leave the truck in town without someone to guard it. Not only were the goods on the truck vulnerable but left alone the wheels could very well disappear. So John advised that I take a passenger with me. This was usually Pieman, but of what use he would have been in an emergency is hard to see. However I did not object to his company and we shared many a conversation, conducted half in English and half in the local dialect.

The Izzu truck developed heating problems and would stop without warning. I would have to pull up and wait until it had cooled down before it would start again. In answer to my complaints about her behavior John would say

"What did you do to make it stop?"

Nothing", I would reply. "She just spluttered and died on me"

"You must have done something" John would say. "Think back"

I would stomp off in a temper after telling him to do his own transporting. To be honest he did try to remedy the fault but he was no mechanic. Once just before I set out on the 200 mile journey through the bush John instructed me that if I had trouble again to

"Take the spanner and gently tap the carburetor here".

I began to question the word "Cherish" in the marriage ceremony.

Eventually the truck was replaced by a Toyota and the fault was found to be a small piece of cotton waste that had been left in the engine by the manufacturers.

At this time the transporting became less as the farm developed but I still had to bring goods for the store which was going from strength to strength.

On one occasion, returning from town, the truck was stoned. As I came down a long straight on the road I saw a crowd of Africans at the road side and as I approached one of them bent down and picked up a stone which he threw at the truck. Immediately the others followed suit and I was forced to run a gauntlet of missiles.

When the first stone hit the truck, my immediate reaction was to slam on the brakes and confront the perpetrators, but after the first hesitation I realized in a flash what a dangerous position I was in. I pushed my foot down hard on the accelerator. The truck responded with a forward bound and I drove on. If I had given into that first impulse, I could so very easily have been murdered by the mob. The thought of what could have happened brought me out in a cold sweat. I thought of the rough hands that would have pulled me from the security of the cab, the smell of the unwashed bodies pressed against mine and, in my mind, I saw the truck burning. My mind refused to dwell on what would have happened to me when I was in the power of the mob. My hands slipped on the steering wheel and my knees started to shake. I had to stop the truck around the next bend as I was shaking so much I couldn't drive. I dropped my head onto my arms and spent several minutes taking deep breaths.

Pieman sitting beside me had turned as white as he would ever be and was as shocked as I was. He kept muttering under his breath and I could smell the fear in the sweat from his body. We sat there until I was calm enough to continue on our way. I began to dread the long trips into town.

On returning to the farm that night, white and very shaken, I told John what had happened and confessed that I was now afraid of driving.

I was hurt by his attitude, for although he sympathized with me, he thought that I was letting my imagination give too much importance to the event.

To be honest there was no point in reporting the incident to the Police. We knew that we could expect no action from them as I would never have been able to identify the Africans.

The next morning, while I was unpacking the goods into the store Viv called in. I was still shaken by the events of the last journey home and unfortunately I told him all about it. Once I had started I could not stop. I told him all my fears about the farm not paying it's way as John was not supervising the labor force.

Viv was very sympathetic and shocked that I should continue to travel in alone and at the first opportunity he spoke to John.

John was furious.

"How could you discuss with someone else our private affairs?" he shouted. "Have you no loyalty at all"

I was now doubly hurt but I was angry too.

"Loyalty?" I shouted back. "I've followed you from pillar to post around this country and worked on your farm harder than any of the other wives."

It made no difference. Shouting at each other would never solve our problems and indeed this one was never resolved. As usual we did not speak for a couple of days and then life went on as before.

Another factor that increased the general feeling of insecurity was the training of a terrorist army in Zambia, to fight on Rhodesian soil. These Africans, often recruited straight out of the bush and of an alien tribe, were being trained in various camps scattered around Zambia. They were often not paid a regular salary and took to robbing and terrorizing the local community. We were fortunate, in Mkushi, we did not have any camps in the vicinity but we were alarmed at the accounts of atrocities being carried out in other parts of the country.

A wealthy European farmer, in the main Lusaka–Ndola road, had been farming in the area for many years and had reared a prize herd of cattle. I had met the family one day when the truck had broken down near their farm and they had kindly come to my assistance.

One evening a group of so called 'Freedom Fighters' had used his prize herd of cattle as target practice and by the time the very irate owner had arrived on the scene, several had been mortally wounded. While confronting the gang the farmer was shot and killed. His wife who ran to his assistance sustained bullet wounds to her eyes and was blinded.

We never did hear if the perpetrators of these crimes were brought to justice. Apart from the very personal tragedy the country could not afford to lose this sort of person who was the backbone of the agricultural economy.

The terrorist incursions into Rhodesia from Zambia forced the Rhodesian Government to close its northern borders with Zambia. No petrol, spares for tractors and cars or fertilizer, or other commodities that were normally imported from the south were allowed in to Zambia. It must be remembered that England had imposed sanctions on Rhodesia but Rhodesia had continued to provide food and fuel to Zambia until now.

Just as important, if not more so, the export from Zambia of her main currency earner, copper, was now seriously curtailed. To the north of Zambia in the Congo a bloody civil war was still raging. In an endeavor to redress this situation the Zambian Government commissioned all trucks of three ton or over to carry the vital copper along the north east road to Dar es Salaam and to return with petrol and diesel in forty four gallon drums. The drums once emptied at depots at Kapiri Mposhi would be returned for refilling to Dar es Salaam.

And so "The Hell Run" came into being. As I have already pointed out this road was nothing but a dirt track. In the dry season it was just one long line of corrugations clothed in endless thick dust clouds. In the rainy season it turned to a muddy stretch of puddles and streams.

The Government did start the construction of a permanent tarred road almost at once but this highway would take years to complete.

The endless convoy of trucks with drums rattling interspersed with the heavy copper lorries did nothing to improve the already deteriorating surface of the road. As they returned with their precious load of drums the fuel dripped from the holes that had been made with the never ceasing jarring from the rough surface of the road. Not only was the fuel lost in this way but the drivers, ever ready to turn a quick penny, sold what they could on the return journey to anyone with ready cash.

In the rains it was not unusual to come across some twenty trucks held up at some impassable stretch of the road. The surrounding trees would have been cut down to line the muddy track but often this was not enough and the traffic was held up until a bulldozer managed to get through and pull the trucks out of the mire.

On one occasion John and Marney on a trip into Lusaka had come across just such an incident.

A very large lorry, carrying copper had become bogged down in the mud blocking the road to traffic from both directions. Unable to progress further and using a fair amount of initiative the African drivers and their helpers had unloaded the copper bars from the truck and laid them in the water logged road in an effort to build a causeway. While this construction was going on the other drivers used the interval to brew up their tea. They were sitting besides their trucks pumping up small primus stoves while the diesel and petrol dripped slowly out of the drums around them.

John and Marney taking in the potential explosive situation at a glance decided to delay their trip to town and returned home.

However, somewhere in the African bush there possibly still remains an expensively copper paved expanse of road!

CHAPTER 18

The school year in Africa runs from January to December as we drew near to the beginning of the next tobacco season, which was roughly August, I realized that Debby was not progressing in her lessons as she should have been. If this was because I was not with her every day or because she was not capable I did not know but as I thought that she really was quite a bright little girl it must have been my teaching. I turned the matter over in my head for a few months. She would be eight the following year in February, and although it was not ideal many of the children went to boarding school at this age. I also hated leaving her and Gavin alone, when I went on my trips to town. The security situation in the country continued to deteriorate and I was frightened. If I sent Debby to school, I felt that she would be safe. But what of Gavin? He would then be alone on the farm. John could so easily have helped in this situation and taken Gavin with him about the farm but when I discussed these matters with him he was quite adamant that Gavin should also go to the Convent in Kabwe. I was unprepared for this. Gavin was still such a little boy. Perhaps John did not feel secure on the farm either and thought that the children would be safer in town. Why would he not discuss the situation with me instead of just laying down the rules?

"Lore is at the school and she will keep an eye on him". John reasoned.

I knew that the Nuns would look after him well and mother him but it was to break my heart when I sent him away. And so the arrangements were made and both Debby and Gavin would start school the following January.

I often wondered why John appeared to openly dislike his son. Was it usual for Fathers to bear a certain animosity towards their sons? I certainly could not see it in Viv's attitude towards his offspring. Gavin appeared to reciprocate these emotions, I wondered if there was an element of jealousy in their relationship. John was certainly harder on Gavin than he was on the girls and expected very much more from him.

On one occasion, we were driving over to Viv and Joan in the gathering dusk. The lights on the truck failed. Without any hesitation John perched Gavin on the front wheel mud guard with a torch and told him.

"keep it shining on the track so that I can see where we are going"

I was appalled and protested loudly. Gavin was only five years old at that time. When Gavin failed to keep the torch trained on the road, John lent out of the window.

"Can't you do anything right? Keep the torch steady" he shouted.

I insisted that John stop the truck and I took Gavin's place after telling him that he had done a good job. I found that it was very difficult to keep my balance on the precarious perch, as we drove over the rough road, never mind keeping the torch trained on the road. John was annoyed with me.

"You always take his part" He said. "Gavin is quite capable of holding the torch. You are much too soft with him".

I could not believe that my husband could treat our son in such an off hand manner but I did not know how to deal with the situation. One needed to be a psychologist to tread the mine field between father and son and I was sadly ignorant in this field. On the other hand Gavin appeared to have very little respect for John.

One weekend we were invited to spend a Sunday with the Dendy Youngs, who farmed a little way from us, and we took a picnic to share by their pool. The usual neighbors, were there, Viv and Joan, with some of their brood, Marney and Nella, who only had one child with them, the others being away at school, and Helen and Des. We made a happy crowd, the usual farming pressures being left behind for the day. The garden was in full bloom and the pool a delight. We swam all day, ate too much and enjoyed the company.

In the late afternoon we started to pack up pleasantly tired from the sun and the relaxing day. The adults were all dressed and having left Gavin in the pool for as long as possible I told him to get out and get dressed. He ignored me. John repeated my request but Gavin had a stubborn streak and ignored John. Raising his voice John shouted at Gavin

"Get out now!"

Gavin looked up at John and replied "Come and get me".

John jumped into the pool fully clothed and pulled his son out after giving him a resounding slap. Later that night as I put Gavin to bed I told him

"Don't ever dare your Father again like that". Unrepentant Gavin replied.

"Huh! I wish I had been in the deep end" I had to turn aside to hide my smile.

In the meantime the new season was upon us. The lands lay ridged and ready for the tobacco seedlings that were being watered and made ready for planting.

I returned from Lusaka with an empty truck. I had gone to fetch fertilizer that should have been delivered onto the farm a month previously.

"There is no fertilizer at the depot" I told John "There might be some next week but they are not sure"

This was a blow indeed as we could not plant out the seedlings with the first rains unless the lands were first dressed with fertilizer. The whole planting program could be seriously delayed.

Because the fuel company could not deliver our diesel for the tractors we had had to buy on the black market. The expense had been enormous.

It did seem that everything was gradually falling apart. However all the farmers were in the same boat and I noticed that when I was at home, John spent much of his time going to the neighbors to discuss the situation.

The farmers on the scheme that we were on did not seem to be getting any assistance from the Department that was running it. It was vital, in this our third year, that fertilizer and fuel were on the farms and ready for use. It was to be a make or break year for most of us.

After several impromptu meetings, of only the men, it was decided to start a Tenant Farmers Association to put their grievances to the Government. These meetings usually took place in the late afternoon on a different farm each time and continued well after dark or until the communal hoard of liquor had been consumed.

A committee was eventually formed but John was not elected chairman as I think he secretly wished. When the committee called for a secretary John volunteered my services. It annoyed me that all the women had been excluded from the first meetings but when there was real work to be done they were considered good enough to be included in the proceedings.

When he told me he said

"There won't be much to do. Only a letter or two" "What about the minutes of the meetings?" I asked. "Oh. You'll have to do those too" was his answer.

And so another chore was added to my workload. I didn't really mind this as I enjoyed the meetings and the break they gave me from the farm but I did resent the dictatorial manner in which my husband volunteered my services.

Of course the job entailed a good deal more than the occasional letter but we were able to get guaranteed deliveries of fuel and fertilizer.

Eventually all was ready for the rains to start. They were late and the land lay baked under a hot relentless sky. The wind, now hot and stifling, removed the last of the leaves from the trees. There was no shade to be found anywhere. The rivers and vleis slowly gave up their moisture to the skies and the soft sandy earth became a dust filled bowl, where there was no grass. The dust devils rushed over the ploughed fields adding to the look of desolation. In the early dawn, before the sun began it's burning, the sky was pale blue with no clouds. As the day wore on, the sky took on a glassy metallic color, and the clouds slowly gathered on the far horizon. They built up into towering giants but with the disappearance of the sun at nightfall they vanished and another day of searing heat followed with a further empty promise of rain in the afternoon.

There was a prevailing smell of hot dust when we walked through the towering golden grasses that shed their seeds at the slightest touch. The birds seemed to have vanished and we missed their song, their silence adding to the ominous atmosphere

As November wore on the heat and dust seemed to intensify – if that was possible. We turned our eyes beseechingly to the dry skies. The days seemed endless.

In the truck my hands slipped on the sweat that had gathered on the hot steering wheel. There was no relief from the open window where the yellow dust spilt in when I passed another vehicle. My skin seemed to have a permanent covering of sand.

Eventually towards the end of the month the winds quickened in the heat of the afternoon and the cloud build up became more acute. Instead of the towering white clouds the horizon was now obscured by a black line from which jagged shafts of lightning emerged. Thunder rumbled in the distance. Slowly, ever so slowly, the black mass drifted ever closer. In the late afternoon the wind increased and with it came the fresh smell of the rain. The trees bent to the onslaught of the wind and the tall grass lay flat on the earth. In the vlei the short grass rippled like waves in the sea. The thunder crashed ever closer and the lightning lit up the whole sky. We could hear the fall of the rain as it came ever nearer.

At last the first fat drops of moisture fell on the parched earth and left soft round marks on the dust. With Gavin and Debby I ran out to feel these first blessed drops on our faces. All at once, it seemed, the heavens opened and the rain lashed down. We had to beat a hasty retreat into the shed as it soon became difficult to breathe. The torrent now collected in puddles that overflowed spilling the water that then swirled away towards the vlei. The drought had broken and in the fresh early dawn the next days planting would once again start.

We moved into the new house just before Christmas. Lore was once again home from school and we had a double celebration. We invited all our near neighbors to a house warming party and Christmas was a very happy time. How different from the first one on the farm when John lay ill behand the tobacco paper and I had to send the children away with their Christmas dinner packed into baskets.

But it was during our party that I noticed that Helen and Des were not really happy. Des was drinking too much and Helen appeared to be miserable. When I drew her aside and asked if I could help her in any way she refused to discuss the matter besides saying that she hated to send her children so far away to school. However I felt that there was more to her depression than that. I felt that I could not pry into her private concerns.

The walls of the house had not yet been painted and in fact never were. John had spent hours building a septic tank for the toilet and we now had a flushing loo as opposed to the open pit that had served us while we were in the shed. At the back of the house there was a Rhodesian boiler that produced our hot water. This consisted of two forty four gallon drums, laid on their sides and built into a brick surround. They lay on top of a grate and a fire would be lit beneath them.

Each child now had their own bedroom but although they went to bed in them, each morning I found all three in Lores bed. Having slept in such close proximity for such a long time, in the shed, they obviously felt insecure by themselves. Eventually they would grow out of this but for the present I ignored it.

The second great event during this time was the installing of electricity to the house and around the barns. When we had arrived on the farm light was provided by hurricane lamps. These had slowly been replaced by the more stylish tilly lamps that also radiated a better glow. They had, however to be constantly trimmed and it was quite a messy chore, to wash the glass shields, every morning, trim or replace the wicks, and fill the lamps with paraffin. Added to this you had to carry a lamp with you when you went from room to room. There was always a candle by our beds in case of an emergency at night but the children were forbidden to light one without either John or me near by. We kept a small paraffin night light in the passage way that merely gave a tiny glow in the darkness.

John had wired the house for electricity during the building and eventually the very large, very heavy, generator arrived on the farm, transported by private contractor.

A special engine room had been built in anticipation of this momentous occasion and the truck reversed up to a few yards from the door of it. The whole labor force was assembled as there was no crane to lift it and this would have to be done by manpower.

Planks were fitted to the back of the truck and the idea was that the engine would be hauled off the truck and then pulled along the ground with ropes. Other planks would be placed in its path as it progressed, much like pictures of the old Egyptians building the pyramids.

Ropes were fitted to the back of the engine to slow it's descent from the truck as well as the pulling ropes in the front.

Eventually all was ready and at a signal from John the slack was taken up and the long line of Africans began their melodious chant. It was a rhythm where on the third count all pulled but put to pertinent words in the local vernacular that I dearly wished I could understand.

The engine slowly descended from the truck and made it's way towards the engine room, the laborers, muscles bulging and sweat streaming from their dark bodies as they strained.

At the entrance to the building it became apparent that a dreadful mistake had been made in the calculation of the width of the door in comparison to the width of the engine. There was now no time to rectify this and as the monster neared the opening it caught the bricks at the side and these came tumbling down. With a shout the laborers dropped the ropes and all ran for safety as the roof slowly collapsed onto the engine.

When the dust had settled John and his right hand man Tarzan, went in to inspect the damage. I was not so brave and knowing my husband's temper I hid behind some convenient bushes.

However, the patron saint of generators must have been around our farm on that day as no permanent damage had been done to the engine, and the bricks and roof were soon replaced.

In a couple of days time when John pushed the "on" button, the lights came on, dimly at first and then brighter as the 'monster' as it became known, slowly gathered momentum. What a joy it proved to be, although we could not run any permanent electrical gadget off it as it only ran during the hours of darkness.

I had already set out the garden and with the rains the big front lawn became a green swathe. The irregular flower beds bordering it held a variety of different colored annuals. Dahlias and zinnias nodded side by side and even delphiniums bloomed in the shade of the natural trees that had been left. Under these trees I had planted bougainvillea that I had grown from cuttings begged from friend's gardens in Lusaka. They would eventually grow and scramble up the trees giving a canopy of color.

I had planted flamboyant and cassia trees from seed and they now lined the driveway into the house. In years to come their red and yellow blossoms would welcome us home. Behind and to the one side of the house was a very large anthill. This I covered with different colored flame lilies that I had scoured from the bush. Unfortunately this was the anthill that erupted one night spilling its soldier ants around the house.

The orchard was now filled with mango, guava, pawpaw, orange and lemon trees, many of them already bearing fruit. As I looked around I was very proud of what we had accomplished in so short a time. I would start to line the farm roads with mango trees that I would grow from the seed of the trees already in the garden, the following year.

The beginning of the school term drew ever closer and I had to prepare Debby and Gavin for this change in their lives. The school clothing lists were very long and expensive. Each child had to take their own bed linen and towels together with long lists of clothes. With the help of the store they would be well kitted out, all items carefully labeled with their names. The girls wore a blue dress but Gavin would go to school in a pale grey safari suit. He was very tall for his age and looked so very sweet in his school uniform. I wondered how he was going to take to the restriction of his uniform as he only ever wore a pair of boxer shorts, a cotton shirt, usually open and sandals. I viewed the six new pairs of underpants with skepticism. His boarding mother, did eventually return to me unused as Gavin had flatly refused to wear them. Both he and Debby appeared to face this forthcoming separation with a certain confidence. . Not so their mother. I spent the days before I took them in to Kabwe hovering between tears and excessively spoiling all three children.

Eventually the fateful day arrived and we packed into the truck. The Nuns advised that I did not visit the children for at least a month, during which time they would hopefully settle down.

Gavin would of course live in a separate building to the girls. At the school I unpacked his clothes and made up his bed for him, then I left him while I performed the same service for a tearful Debby. I hugged all three and kissed them 'Goodbye' hiding my tears and pretending not to see theirs. As I drove away from the school I had to stop around the corner as I could not see out of my sodden eyes. I felt very near to despair. I was sure that life should not be like this. The journey home was very long and silent.

At half term I flew into Kabwe, anticipation lending wings to the truck wheels. They all looked so well and healthy and to my eyes were beautiful. We journeyed home entertained by stories of school and listening to their new songs. On the first homeward journey from school Gavin stole the show with his rendering of

"Hey polly wiggle, hey polly wog, one of these days I'll be a frog'.

I'll kick my legs and swim around with never a splash and never a sound"

We all joined in at the chorus, "umpha, umpha, umpha pha pha". and the little ditty became a regular homeward song.

But the thought that they would soon be returning down this road blighted the sunny day. I never did find a way of making the ride to school happy. Debby would start crying the day before we left the farm and continued all the way in to town. As we came near to the school she would recognize some child and lean out of the window to wave. By the time we drew up at the school gates she was showing signs of excitement and was in a hurry to greet her friends. Sometimes she even forgot to say "Goodbye". Lore took the separation with a certain stoic attitude that I found almost as hard to bear as Debby's tears.

I would return home feeling guilty and very lonely. The house would be too quiet without the sound of their laughter or squabbling and even the dogs seemed to mope and amble listlessly around. To me these partings never became any easier and I would spend most of the homeward trip in tears. I was very unhappy.

At the end of January I received a letter from the Department of Commerce informing me that in accordance with a new law that had been passed, individuals with foreign passports would not, in future be allowed to run commercial enterprises. What they were saying was that as I held a British

Passport, I would not be granted a license to run the store. A Government sponsored Company had been formed and they would come and asses my stock and pay me out at their valuation.

I could not agree to this arbitrary stifling of my enterprise and decided that rather than give it over to them for the mere pittance that they were offering I would let the store run down and eventually close. And so in April the doors closed for the last time, much to the delight of my opposition a few miles down the road.

When we had moved onto the farm, John had decided that the cheapest way to transport goods to the farm was to do it ourselves. The other farmers contracted out to large companies. Well, they didn't have a non paid driver. I am not sure if our way of doing the transporting was any cheaper in the long run as John never costed it out or kept any accounts.

However, in the store, I had instituted a system of credit for our laborers and this money was deducted from their monthly pay, and so helped to reduce our seasonal loan with the bank.

We would also miss this income from the store personally, as much of our foodstuffs end clothes came wholesale through it. Secretly, and after my temper at the dictatorial manner in which it had been carried out had cooled down, I was rather relieved that the responsibility of the store would be lifted from my shoulders.

There had been times when I had actually enjoyed the store. I found that several of the farmers would call in during the day for a chat, as they were passing, Viv being the most frequent. I found myself looking forward to his visits. He always managed to make me feel important and was very free in his compliments. I missed this from John who took me very much for granted. Indeed there were times when I could do nothing right in his eyes and I came to realize that it was at those times when things were not going right for him that I came in for the most criticism.

The season wore on. We were losing tobacco in the fields as the reaping was not going to schedule. I found this hard to understand. John had employed a new 'Boss Boy' or Foreman, but John's continual absence from the fields was taking it's toll. The work force needed the supervision of the Bwana to be effectual.

Grading started. It was a long and tiresome job and when not reaping the whole workforce was employed on it. After an average of seven days curing in the barns the tobacco was removed and stored in bulk bales, where it would pick up a certain amount of moisture. This process was called conditioning. Then when the farmer considered it had enough 'conditioning', each leaf was graded by hand for color and thickness and baled ready for market. For this job the women were also employed.

Much of our tobacco that year came out of the barns black. We never did find out if this was due to too much nitrogen in the fields or to a barn rot caused by uneven curing in the barns. Whatever the cause we lost a great deal of tobacco. It became evident that we would not be able to repay our seasonal loan.

Theft from the farm became very serious. As the maize ripened the Africans from the reserve crossed the road and literally stripped the plants bare. We did put a guard on the fields but confronted with a gang intent on reaping the crop he was powerless.

We did of course contact the police. An African constable appeared on the farm the following week but fully admitted that he was unable to take any action. The police were not welcome in the reserve where the chief's word was law.

Rabies hit the district once again. We were used to these periodic outbreaks of this terrible disease. As a matter of routine all our domestic animals were injected annually as a preventative measure. I immunized our own animals and many of the neighbors' animals as well.

The dogs were not difficult to do but the cats had to be put into a sack and a back leg was pulled through a hole so that I could get a firm grip on it. The day I held these yearly veterinary sessions was usually quite a laugh as the neighbors' dogs and ours usually started to fight and the various cats would set up a caterwaul to deafen anyone around.

When a case of active rabies was discovered all dogs had to be tied up to prevent them roaming. A system had been devised by which their leads were attached to a long wire stretched between two trees so that the animal had a fair range of movement. Naturally the dogs in the reserve still roamed the bush free. The Africans living there refused to let any veterinary officer into the reserve and their animals were never immunized

If our dogs had not been tied up at that time perhaps the most serious incident that year could have been avoided.

Jess was an alsatian bitch who had belonged to some neighbors of ours in Chilanga, George end Mavis Perfect. When they had decided to leave the country they contacted us and asked if we would take the dog to avoid having her put down.

John had picked her up on one of his trips to town and Jess attached herself to him. She followed him everywhere and stood guard over him in the fields. We came to regard her as his shadow.

But on a morning when John went to check on the barns she was tied up because of the rabies scare. As John came around the corner of the barns he found an African removing the roofing from one of the barns. John apprehended the African who then turned around and attacked him. The two men rolled in the dust, both fighting for supremacy. The African was a young man and John was in his fiftieth year and quite frankly the African had the advantage. John was unable to extract himself and Tarzan had to come to his rescue. The African ran off into the bush and John staggered back to the house. When I saw him, his face was puce colored and he could hardly breathe. During the course of the fight John had been bitten very badly in several places on his hand and back but worse than this was the loss of face that he had suffered before the whole labor force.

Although I treated the bites they went septic and John became ill again. This time I had the penicillin ready and we were able to avoid a prolonged sickness. But now, although he would not admit it, John was frightened. He went less and less to the barns and fields. I watched him slowly lose interest in the farm and my heart sank as I realized that once again John was looking for a way out of his responsibilities.

In August John went into the Land Bank, which controlled the finances for the farm on behalf of the Government, to apply for the seasonal loan. We had not managed to repay the whole of the last loan but we still had the maize to reap and we thought that the debit would not be very large.

"They have refused me another seasonal loan", he told me on his return.

With no further explanation he turned away and walked off into the garden. I was left to think this over by myself. Eventually I approached him.

"What are you going to do now?" I asked.

"I don't know" he said. "Everything I try turns to dust"

I did not tell him that I thought that the crop failure was due to the lack of supervision. This was not the time, I thought.

"Do you want to stay on the farm?" I asked. "What else can we do?" he answered.

"Shall I go in and ask Mr. Phiri at the Land Bank?" I pressed.

"I can't see what good that will do. If he wouldn't give it to me, what makes you think that he will give it to you?" he answered "But go if you want to".

"John, it is surely worth a try unless you have another idea. We have no money and there is nothing else that we can do at this stage. The school fees have to be paid and there is no longer any money from the store. Perhaps if we can get another year you might make a success of it. At least it will give us another 12 months to make some contingency plan. We can no longer just up and go as you have in the past."

The following week I drove into Lusaka to the Land Bank and confronted Mr. Phiri. Poor Mr. Phiri! He was a very small, very black African who sat behind a very large desk and was confronted by a very tall European woman who refused to sit down and so towered over him.

In African custom a woman or a supplicant (as I should have been) must always be the lower but in our case because of our respective statures this was impossible and so I chose to stand.

Looking back I am a little ashamed of my intimidating manner but I was fairly desperate and had spent the last few days propping up my courage. I did not like what I had come to do and really did not consider it my place. I had not wanted to come to Mkushi but I had done all in my power to make the venture a success.

Mr. Phiri and I talked for a good half hour and I explained that we had used the proceeds of the store to supplement the wages until the Government had closed it. I needed the money to feed our children and I told him that three years was not long enough to test a farmer on. Added to this was the theft from the fields. I used every argument that I could think of and no one was more surprised than I when I came away from his office with the coveted loan. I think that he was only too glad to get rid of me and probably breathed as big a sigh of relief as I did when I gathered up my papers and muttering profuse thanks made my retreat and left his office.

Returning to the farm I could not believe that I had succeeded. I was elated. Thinking back over the last three years I was also astounded at how my self confidence had grown. When I had married I had been an independent and self–sufficient young woman. In the early years of the marriage, in order to avoid the fights and rows I had submerged my personality in my husband's. His word had become law. This was in accordance with the Church's teaching which I had, over the last few years, begun to question. I could no longer agree that we must all suffer for my husband's shortcomings. There was no gratitude in John's attitude to my help and indeed he appeared to belittle everything that I succeeded in. Now I had been successful where he had failed and I was very proud of myself.

However my balloon was soon burst as far from being pleased that we had received a reprieve John was bitter.

I tried to point out that it was not me who had succeeded but the farm. This attitude made no impression on John and as we approached the coming season my hope that matters would be any different dwindled. He had lost interest in the farm, whether from fright or just plain boredom I didn't know, but I was very familiar with the signs and once again my heart sank. What now? Well, we had another year or possibly eighteen months in which to decide. If anything our position was all the more desperate now.

CHAPTER 19

Suddenly I found myself with time on my hands. This was bad for me as I now had time to dwell on the fact that the children were so far away. If I had only waited a few months more there would have been no necessity for Gavin to be sent away, and with time I was sure that I would have been able to improve Debby's lessons. Debby was doing very well at school and had absorbed her lessons at home better than I had thought. She was also proving to be an excellent swimmer. In fact both girls excelled themselves at the sport.

Both John and I went into Kabwe for the annual swimming gala and shouted ourselves hoarse when the girls won their races. We were very proud of them both.

Because Debby did so well at her swimming John started to take more notice of her. During the Easter holidays a swimming gala was held at the club as part of the holiday entertainment that was always arranged for the children and our girls swept the board. Even in the family race amidst much hilarity and cheating we came in a good second. The girls said that if their father had been a better swimmer we would have won! It said much for the atmosphere in the family that John took this teasing in good spirit.

However Lore was not doing well at the convent. She was now twelve and it was time that she went to secondary school. Did we keep her at Kabwe, where due to the Government policy the Nuns had to take in a larger percentage of Africans to whites and so were forced to take girls of a lower educational standard than their age? Both Lore and Debby had been at multiracial schools from the beginning but in the past the educational standard had been a priority, whereas now we could see the standard dropping rapidly. The only alternative was to send her out of the country to Rhodesia. It was a very hard decision for us as parents to make. Added to this was the fact that Lore had always suffered from homesickness when away from home and if we sent her to Rhodesia we would see less of her than we had been able to while she was in Kabwe.

On one occasion I spoke to Mother Rosa, who was at that time Lore's class teacher and she told me

"Lore is always staring out of the classroom window. When I asked her what she was looking at Lore replied "I'm looking to see if Mkushi is having rain"

Apparently Lore's whole attention was focused on the farm. My heart twisted for my daughter.

Mary's girls went to a private boarding school called Nagel House at Marandellas, which was some 50 miles on the Eastern side of Salisbury and therefore some six hundred miles from Mkushi. It was run by American Nuns and had a good reputation and, I reasoned, if Mary thought it was a good school it must be. Since Mary and Fred had been so successful on their farm, only the best was good enough for their children.

As we would not be able to see Lore at half term or on exit days, it seemed wise to send her there as Mary would look after her at those times. But it was so far away! John was adamant that Lore get the best education that we could give her and it therefore seemed that I had no alternative but to agree that she should be sent to Nagel House.

We discussed the change with Lore who, as always, accepted the inevitable without any argument.

And so I begged a lift from a neighbor who was traveling down to Rhodesia and they dropped me at Karoi. I had not seen Mary and Fred while we were at Mkushi and there was much news to catch up on. Fred very kindly lent me the farm truck and I drove to Marendellas and arranged for Lore to start school there the following January. I was confident that with the new seasonal loan arranged, I would be able to pay the fees for the first year. The year after that? Well as things were at present I could only plan for the year ahead.

The school was set in large well tended grounds, and instead of long depressing dormitories, as in Kabwe, the girls were accommodated in smaller rooms with only four beds to each. Instead of the drab blue of the Convent uniform the girls were dressed in maroon skirts with cream blouses. The Sunday or walking out uniform was a crushed raspberry worn with a straw boater. The food seemed to be of a high standard, which would please Lore as she was very fond of her meals. The sporting facilities seemed good and I came away feeling that if Lore had to be sent away this was the place for her.

The only alternatives were the Dominican Convent in Salisbury, where I had been educated, and which was run on the same lines as the one in Kabwe, or a Government school where she would not receive a Catholic education.

The family problems played on my mind during my trip down to Rhodesia and I turned the situation over and over in my mind and tried to analyze my feelings.

I was definitely a late starter and it had taken me years to realize that my husband would never make a success of any enterprise that he was in sole control of. The shades of my father then loomed very large and I decided that Mum's life was not for me.

I was content to go along with him if only he and I were concerned but now with the children growing up I could no longer close my eyes to his shortcomings. How much was I to blame for always following his lead? Admittedly I had promised to follow him 'For better or worse', but now I began to seriously question the wisdom of following the Church's teaching. Let's face it I was no longer blindly in love with my husband and as I had watched his deterioration and descent into fright and near panic, much of my respect for him had vanished. God knew. I understood what it was like to be frightened but somehow I had always expected him to be stronger. He had never listened to my fears and put most of them down to 'my over active imagination'. Besides this, as I now realized, John would not make a success of the farm. I came to the conclusion that I must now put the children's welfare first.

When I returned to Karoi I started to enquire if I could support the children by myself. Karoi seemed to be the best place to start as I had lost most of my connections in Salisbury and besides I needed the moral support of my sister. I was sure that she would help me in the transitional period.

I started at the school. With my nursing training I would be welcomed as a school matron there. The Headmaster agreed that Debby would join the regular boarders and Gavin being so young would share my room at the school. This would solve the accommodation problem. The Karoi school was only a primary one and as Lore was now older she would not be with us.

The pay was reasonable but because I would not be divorced John would be responsible for the school fees. As he was not in Rhodesia the school fees would be charged as extraterritorial, and therefore much higher than for the Rhodesians, and my pay would not cover these. I was sure that if I took matters into my own hands John would not consent to pay these fees and even if he did agree would he pay on time? I had bad experience of how John just pushed unpleasant matters out of his mind. This information crushed all my plans. Whatever job I managed to get I would never be able to pay the school fees by myself.

What would be the best thing to do? Although I did not discuss the farming situation with Mary and Fred they were very aware that matters were not as rosy as expected.

I decided that I would have to return to Mkushi with my tail between my legs, defeated before I had even started.

I was startled by the welcome I received from John. I had not breathed a word of my intention to leave but he seemed genuinely pleased to have me back and I allowed myself to be lulled into a sense of false security. I suppose that deep down I did not want to have to make the decisions that now faced us.

The grading season had ended and our tobacco, what there was of it, had gone off to the sales. I was well aware that John found grading very boring but I was a little shocked when he informed me that next year, as I no longer had the store, I should take over the task of supervising it. To me this was just more evidence of his loss of interest and I was determined that I would not take on this task.

However life with its twists and turns would solve the problem.

On the surface life appeared to settle down once again. In order to fill my days I joined the ladies in our area at tennis once a week: that was held on Helen and Des's farm. Well it was more a 'hit and giggle' than tennis and I discovered that hitting a ball around the court was a great way of venting one's emotions.

I had joined the local W. I. in our first year but had never taken a very active part; now I was persuaded to represent this group at the annual National Convention that was to be held in Mufalira on the Copper Belt.

Together with Avvy I flew up in John Dendy Young's small plane. We were meant to stay there for three days but both Avvy and I objected to the recommendation of the conference and were told to either shut up or leave. We left.

The cost of living and inflation in Zambia was rising in leaps and bounds. The conference would not allow that this was due in part to the closing of the Southern border and the transporting of all goods from Dar Es Salaam by a rough road. The delegates voted to condemn all small shop owners and urged Government to take steps to ensure that anyone who increased their prices was prosecuted and heavy fines levied. The unfairness of the recommendation (which would no longer affect me) and the fact that women could pass such an unintelligent statement annoyed me intensely and of course I had to stand up and say so. This was the cause of our downfall. The President of the conference, herself a white woman, called me aside and said I was making a political judgment and we were no longer welcome at the Conference.

When we returned to Mkushi John was very angry with me.

"Why now of all times do you have to openly make anti Government statements?" he shouted.

"They were not anti Government" I returned "They were anti conference and not fair."

"Don't you realize that we are living in a black run country and that fairness does not come into the scheme of things. You will have us thrown out" he added.

I did admit that I should not have been so hasty and should have objected less strongly to the recommendation. It appeared to me to be a matter of principle rather than politics. However after my discussion with John I began to realize that I could have put all the Europeans in our block in danger. Indeed people had been deported for less offences than mine in the past.

I resigned from the W. I. However as far as I was concerned it was just one more nail in the coffin.

In May that year, John accepted a lift into Lusaka with a middle aged bachelor called Bill. There was nothing unusual in this as farmers doubled up on trips to town if possible.

They left at day break and were to return that night. John was well aware that I did not like to spend the night alone on the farm with no protection at all.

I kept a meal warm for both men to have when they returned but by midnight there was no sign of them and I rechecked the locks on all the doors and windows in the house. Many of the windows were still not curtained and as I passed one I was sure that I saw a face peering in. Every time that the crickets stopped their steady hum I imagined a stealthy foot tread had passed by. One of the dogs outside started to bark. I was working myself up into a panic and knew that this was the worst thing to do but I could feel an ominous presence around the house. At last summoning my courage I opened the back door and called the dogs into the house. With them beside me in the bedroom I finally settled to sleep. At sunrise, after a restless night I threw the food that I had prepared the previous night away, went out into the morning and started the laborers on the daily tasks that I thought should have been done that day. I had no idea what John's plans were for the week.

At sundown there was still no sign of the men and once again I prepared a meal and endeavored to keep it hot on the wood stove ready for their return. The night repeated the same pattern as the previous one.

Day followed weary day and night followed sleepless night. By now I was convinced that some terrible fate had overtaken the men and that they were lying dead by the road side. In my imagination I had John buried and had sold what I could from the farm and with the children had returned to Karoi.

Because John had been so cross when I had spoken to Viv about the crop failure I hesitated to go to any of the neighbors for help, till the fifth day dawned. Then I drove over to Viv and Joan and surreptitiously enquired if there had been any news. No news is good news I told myself as I returned to the house.

As evening was drawing in John and Bill arrived hale and hearty. John was very clever as he kept Bill in the house till late on. He knew that I would not make a scene with another man present.

I was so angry that I never said a word. I did not ask for an explanation as to why they were late or where they had spent the time and none was given to me but I wondered what my reception would have been if I had done the same thing. I realized that we were just jogging along together and that John probably felt as trapped as I did. The solution could have been to sit down together and talk over the situation but I knew from past experience that John would never listen when I explained my feelings and would not lower himself to discuss our fast failing marriage.

The children came home for the winter holidays and as usual there was now much traveling between farms and the club but the thought that the holidays must end always seemed to me to put a blight on any festivities but these feelings I kept to myself.

The bore hole broke down. Catastrophe indeed. We did have the shallow reservoir, which although usually covered with scum would serve the livestock but with forty laborers and their families, not to mention our own, fresh water was essential.

As usual the neighbors came to our aid and Mantey spent two days with John laboriously pulling up the rods that rode up and down inside the two and a half inch pipes. There was a foot pump at the bottom of the bore hole. At the start of the operation there was no indication of where the fault lay.

A tripod was set up over the bore hole, the engine removed and the rods laboriously pulled up by clamping the top one, moving it up a few feet, fitting another clamp and removing the first. Then the process was repeated until all 120 rods had been lifted in order to raise the foot pump.

The men both black and white sweated and strained in the heat and had to be constantly provided with cool drinks.

In the mean time we had to cart water from Viv's farm on forty four gallon drums. When the bore hole was reassembled and the first water gushed out the whole labor force stood around and cheered.

The new season started.

The lands once again lay ridged and ready for the small plants that were already peeping through the ground in the seed beds. This year we were on time and I hopefully crossed my fingers that the good start would also mean a good ending.

Perhaps it was this false sense of security or maybe just a change in the seasons but I discovered that I was once again pregnant.

At first I could not believe the signs. I was 37 going on 38 years old and surely I should have been in better control by now! With our marriage on such shaky terms it could not have happened at a worse time.

Both John and I were shattered but we gradually grew to accept the situation. Well there was nothing else that we could do.

When the rains came planting started but this year we had a plague of snake bite incidents.

The Africans never wore shoes unless they had progressed up the employment ladder. The boss boy and the tractor drivers boasted dirty white canvas shoes while most of the labor force walked on plastic throng sandals which they called patta pattas, from the noise that they made as the wearer walked.

I had had to deal with snake bite on several occasions, particularly at land clearing times but this year the snakes seemed to lie in the fields just waiting for the unsuspecting victim to tread on them. No one ever knew what kind of snake had bitten them and so it was not possible to tell if it was poisonous or not. I treated them all as if they were.

The laborer would be carried into the homestead. Strict instructions had been given that they were not to walk. I would cauterize the wound and inject the snake bite serum into the unfortunate African. I had set up a bed in the back room of the house and he would lie there where I kept a twenty–four hour watch over him while I plied him with hot drinks etc. I never lost a patient from snake bite but later I was to discover that administering the serum did more harm than good.

The children came home for the Christmas holidays and as usual there was much coming and going between the farms.

Viv and Joan still had the only telephone in the district and the small community had grown used to congregating at their house. Everyone brought cakes, beer, or if there was to be a cook–out meat. The children for the most part ran wild, swimming in their reservoir and generally having a great time.

John and I broke the news of the impending increase to our family and took the jokes of being a little on the elderly side for such high jinks in good humor. Everyone seemed to be happy for us except Lore. She was at a very difficult age, knew where babies came from, and probably thought her parents were above that "sort of thing".

The rains that year were very heavy. It rained for days on end once they had started and settled in. My beautiful lawn disappeared almost over night from some blight that attacked it. We were left with just a muddy expanse of earth in the front of the house.

The mornings usually dawned bright and clear but by afternoon the clouds once again poured their moisture onto the already saturated earth. The rivers rose.

One morning in the middle of January Joan and Viv came over to our farm. Joan had a small puppy with her.

"Roni" she said, "This pup is not well. Please look at it. It was a Christmas present to the children from our Boss Boy"

The statement alone should have put me on my guard but I must have been particularly dense that day. I opened the pup's mouth to look at it's gums and it immediately sank it's teeth into the flesh between my thumb and forefinger. In a flash I realized that the dog possibly had rabies but I could not be sure and so advised that it be locked away in a darkened room until the sickness progressed further.

Within two days the pup had died and because of my fears John Dendy Young flew the carcass down to the veterinary center at Mazabuka. After extensive tests it was pronounced that the brain of the pup showed a particularly virulent form of rabies.

We called a hurried meeting of all in our small community to discuss the position. We really had no idea how to deal with the situation. Then one of the men remembered that a couple of hundred miles to to the north of us the World Health Organization had set up a base camp, more or less on the border with the Congo. It was decided that a couple of the men and myself should travel up to it and discuss the problem with them

And so the next day in the early morning we set out. The European in charge of the clinic was an American and he could not have been more helpful once we had explained our situation and shown him the letter from Mazabuka.

He advised that anyone who had remotely come into contact with the saliva of the dead pup must be inoculated with a duck embryo vaccine that he supplied. He added full instructions on administering the injections and with a cheerful wave and a farewell 'Good luck' from him we took our leave.

We returned to the block and held another meeting. Most of the children were due to return to their schools within a few days. Some who went to school in South Africa had already left.

These schools had to be informed and told to arrange the necessary injections. It took a whole day to contact them by phone. The remainder of us should start the treatment on the following day. The injections would be given into the stomach and all would be obliged to have one a day for fourteen days. This meant that the children would be late in returning to school, not that they had any objection.

It was arranged that we would all meet at a different house each day to try and dispel the apprehension the children were feeling.

My own position was somewhat different. I was now three months pregnant and not sure if my baby would be affected by the injections.

Helen Straw had been a nurse but was leaving for the south almost immediately. She agreed to postpone her journey and start the injections the next day while I took a quick trip into Lusaka to consult a doctor there.

He was not very helpful.

"The baby is over three months" he said. "And so should possibly be alright but I doubt that you will be able to carry it. You must have the injections but you will in all probability abort the baby. Unless there is trained help where you live you are putting your life in danger. Come into hospital now and I will remove the baby".

This I couldn't do. Although John was not with me I knew that he also would never agree to an abortion. To us that was murder. I could not kill this tiny scrape of precious life that was lying trustingly inside me.

And so I returned to Mkushi and started on the daily inoculating of our community. Joan's house servant and cook also had to be injected bringing the total to 25 persons. John injected me until he discovered that he couldn't bring himself to do it at which time I injected myself.

We had been warned to watch out for any sign of a reaction from the vaccine but all appeared to be strong and healthy at the end of the fourteen days except for Gavin. He ran a slight temperature and an annoying cough that kept him awake at nights; whether this was the result of the injections or just an ordinary cold I didn't know, but I decided that he must stay at home until he was better.

All the children departed for school. Lore and I managed to get a lift to Karoi and Fred once again lent me his farm truck and we continued on to Marrandellas to Lore's new school. In future it was arranged that she would travel by a bus that had been organized by people on the Copperbelt who sent their children to the same school or others in Rhodesia.

215

As usual it was a sad farewell accompanied by loads of tears, both of us trying hard to hide them under false smiles. Her letters came back to the farm full of accounts of the wonderful food at the school, and on the surface she appeared to be settling down well.

Back at Mkushi the rains continued. The rivers rose and our small community was isolated by bridges being washed away on our main access roads.

John Dendy Young, in his small plane, took Gavin back to school for me. Far from being thrilled by flying as I had thought he would be he was once again grief stricken. How long could I continue with these terrible partings.

Gradually the rains eased off. Reaping began and the barns once more filled up.

I succumbed to a peculiar lassitude and seemed to withdraw from events around me. John was very solicitous and caring and I basked in his unusual attention. I took very little interest in the farm and seemed to spend my days in a trance. I don't think that this condition was induced by the rabies injection. Indeed these seemed not to have had any affect on me at all. Certainly the little life inside me had decided that she would stay warm and comfortable where she was.

In the warm evenings, after the days work, John and I would sit on the replanted front lawn and listen to the old radio that we had carted around the country with us. On Sunday nights the B. B. C. overseas program included an hour of songs by Moira Anderson.

Her lovely voice came over the still air of the African night drowning the usual sounds of the frogs and crickets. These few months would remain in my memory as some of the happiest in my marriage.

On several occasions we saw the 'sputnik' travel across our skies.

April arrived almost unexpectedly and Lore was due back for the holidays. Her bus would stop at Kabwe at about 10 o'clock on a Friday morning. We were up very early that day and set off in high expectations to fetch her. I had written that we would meet her in Kabwe rather than Kapiri Mposhi as John had some business to do there. She never received this letter.

As we passed through Kapiri Mposhi, on our way to Kabwe, we were stopped by an armed guard who searched our truck.

"There must be some sort of scare on" John said but we thought nothing of it as these searches had become a way of life and occurred with monotonous regularity. They seemed to be there merely to annoy the travelers.

In Kabwe, the business completed, we waited, and waited for the bus to arrive, all sorts of mishaps being imagined. Finally after we had made several enquiries we were told that the bus had already passed through. How we had missed it we couldn't understand.

Our informant told us "There was trouble at the border and all the children were taken off the bus at gunpoint. It was only by the quick thinking of the teacher in charge who bribed the guard that they were allowed to continue. Apparently the border is to be closed again"

My heart rose up into my mouth, and I was in a fever of impatience to see my daughter and assure myself that she was safe and sound.

We drove back to Kapiri Mposhi as fast as the truck would go, panic hovering on the horizons of our minds.

As we came to the top of the hill just before the town we were once again stopped by the armed search guard. I couldn't wait for the long question and answering session that I knew would follow before he allowed us to proceed. Seeing a small pink figure in the distance I got out of the car and ran down the road, ignoring the shouts of the guard.

He followed close behind me, waving his automatic rifle and shouting at me to stop. John slammed the truck into gear and joined in the chase expecting to pick his dead wife off the ground.

When I had my daughter in my arms I did stop and explained the situation to the guard. He could now see that a heavily pregnant woman and a young girl of 12 were no threat to the security of Zambia. With much shouting of threats and waving of his rifle he withdrew.

This incident frightened me and I think that John underneath his tough exterior was also worried. Thoughts of what had happened in the Congo to young girls filled my mind and my imagination ran riot.

We collected Debby and Gavin from the Kabwe convent for the school holidays and at the same time I registered with the hospital and had my first anti–natal examination. This was done by a very inexperienced young black doctor, who although I protested decided to try and turn the baby. It was much too early for this and and as I lay on the dirty sheet I decided that I would give birth on the farm rather than come into this germ infested hospital.

In all honesty I cannot blame the staff who were suddenly left to cope when the Europeans left in a drove. In time matters did settle down and improved.

The incidents of the sudden departure of Europeans from the country had been taking place over the last couple of years. Some were deported, like the family of one young schoolboy who was found defacing a poster of President Kaunda. Others just packed their bags and left within twenty four hours.

While most of the remaining white population thought incidents like this were ridiculous, they never–the–less brought home to everyone how insecure their tenure was. Several people just packed their bags and left while others waited until they could sell their houses to a growing affluent African population usually in the Government service. It became commonplace when returning to Lusaka to discover that friends had just left with no forwarding address. It must also be confessed that the departing Europeans took what they could by fair or foul means. The Government had restricted the amount of currency anyone leaving the country could take with them and so most had to resort to underhand ways to remove their assets.

CHAPTER 20

I stood by the loading bay and watched as the last of the tobacco was loaded onto the contract lorry. When all twenty bales were secured the driver took his seat and the truck slowly took off, taking with it our hopes. It was only when the truck had disappeared and the dust had settled that I turned away and walked back to the house.

The tobacco was going into the auction sales in Lusaka. These were held for three or four months every year under the strictest security. Only the grower was allowed into the sales and so I was banned from these, to us, vital sales. I could not understand why this security was in force. I had often attended the tobacco sales in Rhodesia, before U.D.I. and listened in awe as the auctioneers hurried down the long lines of tobacco bales intoning their peculiar chant that only the trained ear could understand and followed by a host of buyers, clerks and growers. In Rhodesia, now that sanctions had been imposed by Britain, the strictest security surrounded their sales as the Rhodesians strove, with quite a measure of success, to break them. But there were no such restrictions in Zambia.

John went into the sales alone and our tobacco sold well, what there was of it. That was the trouble. Most had ended up in my compost pit as it came out of the barns black again.

When John came home the following day we calculated the results of the sale and realized that once more there would be no hope of repaying the whole of the seasonal loan and as the seasonal debt mounted I could not see how we would be granted another for the next year and in all conscience could we even request one from Mr. Phiri at the Land Bank. We had heard that African farmers had run up debts worth thousands of Kwacha and had no hope of repaying them. They were automatically given another when they were members of the ruling political party but this was not for us.

Theft from the fields of maize continued. On one occasion while walking in the lands we found the tracks of a very large truck that had obviously been used to cart the maize away. The husks of the mealies are usually left on the plant to dry until August or September to prevent them from getting mold. John decided to reap early to try and save the crop from the marauders. We stored the still wet husks in the barns to dry them out instead of leaving them in the fields for another three or four months. The yield was good and we pinned our hopes on the money from this crop enabling us to at least pay the school fees in the year.

The two cats that we had brought to the farm had matured into fine adults. Both had been neutered before we left Chilanga and were real family pets. Pan was a ginger and white tom who was partial to hunting trips. He often stayed away over night and on returning would call out to us as he came up the front vlie. Whoever was in the house at that time would then rush to welcome him home with a saucer of milk and a lot of love. So when he did not return home one evening in time for his evening meal it caused no real concern, but as the days passed and there was still no sign of him I began to worry. The whole family scoured the surrounding bush but there was no sign of him. The labor force was alerted but as day followed day we eventually had to acknowledge the fact that Pan would not be returning. Within a couple of weeks Dora disappeared and never returned. He had never done this before as he was a cat who liked his home comforts. I remembered how the Mau Mau in Kenya used to kill cats and put them outside the houses of their victims to frighten them.

Perhaps more alarming although less heart rending, the sheep started to disappear. On that Monday afternoon when they were bought in for their weekly spraying and dosing the count was down by one. The next week two were missing. The herdsman swore that he did not know what had happened to them. We decided that we would have to deduct the cost of the animals from his pay as the carcasses were never found. The herd boy then disappeared which we thought was probably a confession of his guilt. Laborers often disappeared back into the bush if they did not like the foreman or the task they were put on or if someone had put 'muti' outside their huts.

The problem of what to do with the remaining sheep was a knotty one. I felt that it was no use taking on another herdsman and there were no fences on the farm in order to put the sheep out to pasture. It would be utterly useless to appeal to the police for help. They were powerless against the might of the local chief and were very reluctant to come to our part of the district. The chief reigned supreme

As a purely temporarily measure I asked Pieman to herd the sheep for a short while. He was very reluctant to take on this task and I thought that I saw fear in his eyes when he agreed. He was the only laborer that I felt I could trust and seeing his reluctance I realized that my gardener knew more than he was prepared to tell me. For his own safety I did not press him for an explanation. It was also a step down in the labor ladder for him.

I decided that I could not just stand by and watch the remainder of the herd 'disappear' possibly over the road into the reserve and so I calculated the value of the sheep several of which were with lambs and put them up for sale. We were desperate for the money anyway. And so they were sold. On the day when a farmer from the top of the block arrived to collect them I handed over all the stock records and watched as another of my enterprises came to an end I was very depressed. Once more the country had beaten me. I could not shake off the idea that the Chief had a hand in this and possibly in the disappearance of the maze from the fields. However there was no method by which we could prove this and I was forced to concede defeat again. There was nobody that we could turn to for help.

Because it was the school holidays and to get away from the ever depressing money troubles we agreed to travel up to the top of the block to spend the day with Paddy Barrett and his mother.

There was another guest for lunch that day. A businessman from the Copper Belt. He regaled us with stories of how various Europeans had managed to circumvent the very astringent currency regulations that were in force and get their money out of the Country.

The Zambian Kwacha had been devalued drastically and was not welcomed for exchange by the banks outside the country. The Zambian Government had insisted on a take of over 51% of the rich mining companies and overseas investment fell. The price of copper had already fallen drastically on the world markets due to external influences unrelated to Zambia. As copper was Zambia's main foreign currency earner the economic stability of the country was on a steady downward curve. Bribery and corruption had become the order of the day.

The men as usual went off to the fields to discuss the crop and I was left with old Mrs. Barrett to prepare lunch but in the weeks to come I would remember the businessman and realize the effect that his visit had on our lives.

Mrs. Barrett, had bad eyesight. In fact she was nearly blind and wore thick glasses. This in no way restricted her from 'caring' for her son. Her grey wispy hair fell over the heavy frames that hung on the end of her rather large nose and was brushed impatiently aside by hands that were mottled by age spots, to be restricted under the old brown hair net that covered her head. But her faded blue eyes twinkled with the pleasure of unexpected guests and she did all that she could to make the day memorable.

The lunch was a collection of cold meats and salads from the garden but the old lady had decided to make a rice pudding for the children. I stood in the kitchen with her as she prepared the meal and listened as she rambled on. I have often found that lonely people, once they have a captive audience, tend to talk continuously without waiting for any answer from their companion. As no reply was expected of me I watched in silence as the rice was put into the baking dish. She then reached up to the top shelf in the pantry and removed a jar with what looked like some round stones in it. She removed one and proceeded to grate it onto the top of the pudding.

"I was surprised to find that Paddy had these nutmegs" She said. "They must have been here since his wife left but they will still be good. They don't go off" she added.

They did not look at all like nutmegs to me but I thought that as they were old they had possibly changed in color from the usual nutmeg brown to a moldy green. I decided to abstain from the pudding but there was no way in which I could stop the children from having it without embarrassing the old lady.

"Well" I thought, "What doesn't kill fattens and a bit of moldy nutmeg would not hurt them".

After we had finished lunch and the dishes had been cleared away we sat on the veranda drinking coffee. The children went to play in the garden and the adults talked on in desultory manner in the heat of the afternoon. The conversation came around to illnesses and operations.

Paddy informed us that a couple of years ago he had had his gall bladder removed. He spoke with obvious pride of the amount of stones that had been taken from it.

"I still have them" he said with some satisfaction. "They are in a bottle on the top shelf in the pantry."!!

Unfortunately when Paddy said this I had just taken a mouthful of coffee and I very nearly choked on it. After the ensuing back slapping and gasping I noticed that Mrs. Barrett had become very quiet and then start to bustle around clearing away the coffee mugs. Later as I went through the kitchen on my way to the vegetable garden at the back of the house ,to check on the children, I glanced up to the top shelf in the pantry but the bottle of 'nutmegs' had disappeared.

It was once again the start of a new school term and we took Debby and Gavin into Kabwe. Lore would leave the following week. Because of the events at the border when Lore had returned from school in April we had decided that for the time being at least we would have to transport her to and from her school ourselves.

After the usual tearful goodbyes John and I continued into Lusaka to the Land Bank. There was no hope of a further seasonal loan Mr. Phiri told us. This time I knew it would do no good to try and brow beat him. We sat in a cafe after the dreadful interview and worked out the finances that we had left. We had already sent the check for Lore's school but the Convent in Kabwe had not been paid.

We returned to the Convent in Kabwe and explained the situation to the sisters. We offered then the title deeds of our land in Lusaka the value of which would more than cover any outstanding debt to the school, but because title to any land belonging to expatriates (as we were considered to be) was no longer secure the sisters would think it over. The sisters were very kind which made the interview all the more embarrassing. I desperately wanted to take Debby and Gavin home with me but I was persuaded by John and the nuns that as my pregnancy was now quite far advanced it would be wiser to leave them at school. We had both found the interview very humiliating and I was in tears most of the time.

When we returned to the farm that night Pieman came to the back door to see me. Someone had placed 'muti' outside his hut and he was a very frightened man.

I tried to joke about it and said that it was because he couldn't keep his hands off the women.

"No Nkoshi" he asserted. "There have been no women in my hut for a long time now".

I tried to reassure him and let him sleep in the back room of the house that was kept as a store come hospital ward if needed to keep a watch on any sick laborer

The following morning while helping with the loading of the truck an empty drum fell on Pieman's bad leg. He fell off the truck with a scream and lay in the dust whimpering, obviously terrified. I could not find anything wrong with his leg except perhaps extensive bruising. But Pieman could not walk. He was convinced that he was now bewitched and unless he left the farm he would die. I promised him that as we were leaving to take Lore back to school in two days time I would take him with us into Lusaka and leave him at the hospital. In the meantime he remained in the back room of the house, his head covered with his blankets and it was difficult to make him take any food. His skin had lost its luster and turned a mottled grey color. A rank odor of fear surrounded him.

Now that I was now seven months pregnant John would not let me drive the long distance to Marandellas, to take Lore back to school and I was reluctant to remain on the farm alone and so the three of us plus Pieman set out on that Saturday morning in the early hours. The dogs, Foggy, the spaniel, Jess, John's shadow, and Boots, who had mothered Doodle were left in the charge of Mwanza the cook, who was used to them. We would break our journey at the farm in Karoi for a night.

As we passed through Lusaka on our way south we dropped Pieman off at the hospital. I saw the African doctor in charge and explained the situation to him. He knew only too well the power that the Ngangas and witchcraft had over the bush African. Pieman had improved as we got further from the farm but was still very weak. His ready smile no longer lit up his face. We left him with enough money to tie him over until we would pick him up on our return and tried desperately to reassure him.

I confess that I felt very sad at leaving him there and our goodbye was a rather lengthy one. I could not rid myself of the premonition that I would not see my old friend again and indeed this was to prove only too true.

We still hadn't settled the problem of where my 'bump' was going to be delivered. I refused to be delivered in Kabwe as I was sure neither of us would survive the ordeal and although I had bravely stated that I would have the baby on the farm the more I thought of it the more I realized that John would not have been able to help me. He couldn't give me the rabies injections so I was sure that he would not be able to deliver a baby.

225

Helen Straw was a trained midwife but she had not returned from South Africa and we now all doubted that she ever would. Des had not made any statement that their marriage was over but his drinking continued with Helen's prolonged absence and his farm was rapidly going down hill.

At Karoi, where we stopped for the night with Mary and Fred we explained the situation. Although the country was at war I felt secure here. There did not seem to be the brooding ominous atmosphere that prevailed in Zambia and everyone was optimistic.

On our way through we called in at the Government hospital at Sinola to enquire if they would undertake the delivery and were told that they would do it with pleasure. But as we were resident in Zambia we would have to pay an exorbitant sum.

Well we did not have that amount of money and even if we did have it we would not be able to get permission to transfer it out of the country.

We continued on to Marandellas in a very somber mood and I began to think that Kabwe was to be the place of the birth. My skin shrank at the thought. Was I making too much of the situation? Gavin's birth had been so long and difficult and he was so ill after it that I was convinced that I would need expert care. John offered no opinion but was caring and loving and I basked in his unusual attention.

Another parting as we left a tearful Lore at school and made our way back to Karoi. Mary had been busy during our trip to Marandellas and greeted our return with the news that the hospital at Mangula, which was run by nuns, would deliver my baby for a fraction of the cost of the Government hospital. The family decided that I should remain at Karoi until the birth and in the meantime I would have some much needed antenatal examinations.

Mangula was a mine community situated about ninety miles from Karoi. Everything was run to perfection as had been the copper mines in Zambia when under the control of the last Government.

The hospital was clean and modern and the sisters couldn't have been kinder. There was a resident doctor although all the sisters were trained midwives. I felt safe and secure for the first time for many months and although I would have to remain in Karoi for the remaining six weeks of my pregnancy, while John returned to our farm, I was content. I realized that there was nothing I could do about our precarious financial situation until this baby had been born and for the sake of the baby if not for myself I had to let events take their course.